HONEY FOR
A CHILD'S HEART

BOOKS BY GLADYS HUNT . . .

Does Anyone Here Know God?
Don't Be Afraid to Die
Honey for a Child's Heart
MS Means Myself

HONEY FOR A CHILD'S HEART

GLADYS HUNT

ZONDERVAN
PUBLISHING HOUSE OF THE ZONDERVAN CORPORATION
GRAND RAPIDS, MICHIGAN 49506

Honey for a Child's Heart

Copyright © 1969, 1978 by Zondervan Publishing House
Grand Rapids, Michigan

Revised Edition   1978
Sixteenth printing   November 1978

Library of Congress Cataloging in Publication Data

Hunt, Gladys M
  Honey for a child's heart.

  Bibliography: p.
  1. Books and reading for children.   2. Children—
Religious life.   I. Title.
Z1037.H945 1978   028.5   78-3488
Paper: ISBN 0-310-26381-6
Cloth: ISBN 0-310-26380-8

Printed in the United States of America

To
Mark,
a delightful companion
in adventures

CONTENTS

INTRODUCTION

FEW THINGS are more important for a child than to discover
the joy of reading. Give him a love of reading, and you have
given him not only the most satisfying and useful of all
recreations but also the key to true learning. The home is
still the greatest educational force, and parents who make
reading attractive contribute immeasurably to their children's intellectual, emotional, and spiritual development.
Forty-one years as a headmaster have convinced me that a
genuinely educated person is one who knows how to read
and who keeps on reading throughout his life. As Matthew
Arnold said, "Culture is reading."

In *Honey for a Child's Heart*, Gladys Hunt has written a
small book with a big potential. Her suggestions will do

much to lift the cultural level of many a Christian home. Moreover, her practical and lively discussion of the place of the Bible in the family tells how parents can help children gain a life-long love for Scripture. What she says about reading aloud all sorts of literature brings memories of many a Sunday evening in my home at Stony Brook when, after chapel, boys crowded our living room as I read to them before the open fire.

Mrs. Hunt's tastes are broad. Her prose suggestions, which include A. A. Milne, Hugh Lofting, and Lois Lenski, range from Bunyan and Defoe through Dickens, Kipling, and Stevenson to C. S. Lewis, Conan Doyle, Buchan, E. B. White, Thurber and Tolkien. Among her poetry recommendations are Lear, Blake, Masefield, Sandburg, and Frost.

In writing this guide to the enjoyable use of books in family life, Gladys Hunt may well have made herself the benefactress of many a home. And if my enthusiasm for her persuasive little book encourages parents to act upon its advice, I shall be happy indeed.

FRANK E. GAEBELEIN

Books are like people:
    fascinating, inspiring, thought-provoking,
some laugh,
some meditate,
    others ache with old age, but still have wisdom;
some are disease-ridden,
some deceitful;
    but others are a delight to behold,
and many travel to foreign lands;
some cry, some teach, others are lots of fun.
    they are excellent companions,
and all have individuality—
Books are friends.
What person has too many friends?

Playing Pooh sticks.

1.

BEQUEST OF WINGS

"I'M GOING to play in the Hundred Acre Wood," said the small boy who lived at our house.

I knew what he meant and where he was going, and so I said, "Fine. If you see Owl, be sure to ask him about Eeyore's tail."

We knew about Eeyore, Pooh, Piglet, Owl, and Christopher Robin. We had met them in a book[1] together, and our life would always be richer because they had become our friends. To this day I feel sorry for anyone who hasn't made their acquaintance.

That is what a book does. It introduces us to people and

---

[1]A. A. Milne, *Winnie the Pooh*.

places we wouldn't ordinarily know. A good book is a magic gateway into a wider world of wonder, beauty, delight, and adventure. Books are experiences that make us grow, that add something to our inner stature.

Children and books go together in a special way. I can't imagine any pleasure greater than bringing to the uncluttered, supple mind of a child the delight of knowing God and the many rich things He has given us to enjoy. This is every parent's privilege, and books are his keenest tools. Children don't stumble onto good books by themselves; they must be introduced to the wonder of words put together in such a way that they spin out pure joy and magic.[2]

I used to have an eloquent old journalism professor who would often exclaim rapturously, "Oh, the beauty and mystery of words! What richness can be conveyed by those who master them!" And while we jokingly recounted his dramatic incantations to our friends, we ourselves coveted the mastery of words, the symbols which convey ideas. We knew that what he said was true.

Take all the words available in the human vocabulary and read them from the dictionary, and you have only a list of words. But with the creativity and imagination God has given human beings, let these words flow together in the right order and they give wings to the spirit. Every child ought to know the pleasure of words so well chosen that they awaken sensibility, great emotions, and understanding of truth. This is the magic of words—a touch of the supernatural, communication which ministers to the spirit, a gift of God.

We cannot underestimate the use of words in creative thought! Proverbs says, "A word fitly spoken is like apples of gold in pictures of silver." The right word in the right

---

[2]Magic: Any extraordinary or irresistible influence. *The Random House Dictionary.*

BEQUEST OF WINGS / 15

place is a magnificent gift. Somehow a limited, poverty-stricken vocabulary works toward equally limited use of ideas and imagination. On the other hand, the provocative use of the right words, of a growing vocabulary gives us adequate material with which to clothe our thoughts and leads to a richer world of expression.

What fun it is to encourage a personal awareness of words in a child—the delight of sound, the color and variety of words available to our use. I am not suggesting vocabulary drills which teach by rote the meaning of large words. That is quite different than feeling the beauty of words. Books, the right kind of books, can give us the experience of words. They have power to evoke emotion, a sense of spiritual conviction, an inner expansion that fills a child to the brim so that "the years ahead will never run dry."

Books and experience go together. I delight in remembering the night we stayed late after a family picnic along an isolated lake in the north woods—far past normal bedtime for children. We watched the rosy glow of the sunset color the sky on the far side of the lake and darken the silhouettes of the trees. We felt the sand shed its warmth and take on a damp coolness. And then darkness came. We sat around the campfire and listened to the sounds of the night. Young ears picked up things older ears hadn't heard. What we heard we tried to express in words.

Deep-voiced bullfrogs far away, anxious peepers closer by, the gentle lap of the water on the shore, the loon crying in the distance, the crackle of the wood in the fire, the sparks going upward like brief fireflies. And then, as though it were a special gift from God, a whippoorwill, a shy bird usually heard only from a distance, lighted in the bush just behind us and startled us with his clarity of song. Later we watched the moon rise over the trees before going home. We felt beauty: we heard and saw it. We tried to couch the experience in words. Chatter does not enrich;

the right words do. Well-chosen words need only be few in number, and they help store away the pleasure of the adventure.

We have often awakened a small boy at midnight to see the marvel of the northern lights. We have stood on hillsides and described the numerous shades of springtime greens across the landscape. It's a marvelous game of awareness and words.

It's a game that can be played anywhere at odd moments. *How do you think a barn in Nebraska looks?* One child may answer, "Red, with cows around it." Another may say, "Gray and lonely, with no trees near." A third child may light up and say, "The barn looks gray and tired, weathered from the summer's blast of heat and weary from icy winds that blow across the flat plains in winter."

Each answer is a good one. Yet those who saw less will be pleased by the contributions of those who saw more in their minds. They will sense the living substance of a touch of imagination and try to increase their own awareness. You may be thinking at this point, *I handle words so poorly myself. How can I help my children?* This game will teach you as well and bind you to your children as you share what we call "imaginings."

Try other questions: How does a summer night sound? How does a rainy day feel? What does a kindergarten child look like on her way home from school? I have done this in the classroom. Some children's contributions were dull and uninspired, some were hopeful, others had the bright shine of originality. But each child saw the "possibility of words." Natural gifts may differ and, like any other game, contributions should never be the only measure of a person's success. This is only one way of animating the mind in creative effort. But it will help train the ear to listen and the heart to feel beauty and emotion as it comes out in stories that the children later read. The benefits work both ways.

Reading aloud with two teen-age boys this summer, we discussed together the elements of writing which made the story so special. They went back through the chapter and found phrases that spelled out beauty like this, "I feel like spring after winter, and sun on the leaves, and like trumpets and harps and all the songs I have ever heard!" The words fairly ring with joy! I covet for both of these boys the ability to use language with the mastery of the author (J. R. R. Tolkien) whose book we were reading

Since words are the way we communicate experiences, truth, and situations, who should know how to use them more creatively than Christians? The world is crying out for imaginative people who can spell out truth in words which communicate meaningfully to people in their human situation. And of all people on earth, committed Christians ought to be the most creative for they are indwelt by the Creator. Charles Morgan speaks of creative art as "that power to be for the moment a flash of communication between God and man." That concept opens up our horizons to a glimpse of God-huge thoughts, of beauty, of substance beyond our cloddish earthiness, of the immensity of all there is to discover.

Yet, tragically, Christians often seem most inhibited and poverty-stricken in human expression and creativity. Part of this predicament comes from a false concept of what is true and good. The fear of contamination has led people to believe that only what someone else has clearly labeled Christian is safe. Truth is falsely made as narrow as any given sub-culture, not as large as God's lavish gifts to men. Truth and excellence have a way of springing up all over the world, and our role as parents is to teach our children how to find and enjoy the riches of God and to reject what is mediocre and unworthy of Him.

Children are the freest and most imaginative of creatures. They love the fun of words and have a spectacular ability to learn. We must respect their eagerness and competence by introducing them to good books. I am frankly excited by the potential of books to build a whole, healthy, spiritually alert child who has the capacity to enjoy God and be useful to Him.

Emily Dickinson has winsomely captured the spirit of this:

> He ate and drank the precious words,
> His spirit grew robust,
> He knew no more that he was poor,
> Or that his frame was dust.
> He danced along the dingy ways
> And this bequest of wings
> Was but a book. What liberty
> A loosened spirit brings![3]

Any good book can be used by God in a child's development, for a good book has genuine spiritual substance, not just intellectual enjoyment. Books help children know what to look for in life. It is like developing the taste buds of his mind as a child learns to savor what he sees, hears, and experiences and fits these into some kind of worthwhile framework.

What is unfamiliar becomes close and real in books. What is ridiculous helps children see the humor in their own lives. Sympathetic understanding is a generous by-product of sharing the emotions of others in stories. Books are no substitute for life, but a keener pleasure comes to life because of books.

When you've walked across a field with an eight-year-old who comments on the "smell of sweet grass in a sunny pasture," then you'll understand what I mean. Or, "Dandelion stems are full of milk, clover heads are loaded with nectar, and the refrigerator is full of ice-cold drinks. Summer is very nice." Then you hear the words you read from *Charlotte's Web* come back to your own daily experience

---

[3] *The Poems of Emily Dickinson* (New York: T. Y. Crowell, 1964), p. 20.

and agree, "Yes, summer is very nice."

This savoring of life is no small thing. The element of wonder is almost lost today with our mechanical devices and space-age living. To let a child lose it is to make him blind and deaf to most of life. Children have marvelous elasticity of mind. Fancy a child who hasn't met a dragon or a unicorn! Imagine a child who doesn't speculate about what small creatures might live in a hollow tree or rocky crevice! That's the stuff a sense of wonder may feed on, but when the child is older he will respond with the same sensitivity to a lovely sentence from Monica Shannon's *Dobry*: "Snow is the most beautiful silence in the world."

I have never been able to resist the appeal of a child who asks, "Read to me, please?" The warm security of a little person cuddled close, loving the pictures which help tell the story, listening to the rhythm of the words, laughing in all the right places as the policeman stops Boston traffic for the mother duck and her family in Robert McCloskey's *Make Way for Ducklings*. Or the safe, soothing feeling of Margaret Wise Brown's *Good Night Moon*, or the wonder of Alvin Tresselt's *White Snow, Bright Snow*.

But the pleasure doesn't end with small children who like to sit on your lap. Growing-up children are just as much fun. Reading Laura Ingalls Wilder's books of pioneer adventure on the prairie, our family could feel the warm cabin, smell the freshly baked bread, hear the blizzard raging outside, and experience with Laura the close family feeling of Pa's singing and fiddling by the fireside. The love and gaiety of the Ingalls home were shared in our home, and we had a quiet confidence in a family's ability to surmount dangers and hardships.

Books *do* impart a sense of security. Children meet others whose backgrounds, religions, and cultural ways are unlike their own. They come to accept the feeling of being different, and fear, which is the result of not understanding, is removed. Geography invades our living rooms as children visit families from other countries, and the world seems quite friendly.

Facing failures and tragedies with the characters of a story may vicariously give children the experience of courage and loyalty. Weeping with some and rejoicing with others—this is the beginning of a compassionate heart.

Courage is transmitted by heroes like *Johnny Tremain* and even the comical Reepicheep in *The Voyage of the Dawn Treader*. Valor does not belong to an exclusive race of supermen. It is within the hearts of those who are committed to truth and honor, the kind of heroes with whom one can identify. Children have loved the biblical Daniel, David, and Joseph for these same reasons and have gained deeper understanding of the relationship of courage to faith.

One of my young friends read *Call It Courage* at least four times last year when he was nine. In transition between being a *child* and being a *boy*, he needed a model for his new manhood. This book fed his heart with ideals and integrity in such practical ways that it is difficult to measure its influence. He said, "It made me feel brave and strong!"

Every parent who reads with children and every teacher who shares books knows the wistful sigh that accompanies the request for "one more chapter." Because I love reading so much myself, I can never be too harsh when asked, "May I just finish this chapter?" even when I suspect that they are only on page two. I remember with special fondness the English teacher in my high school who sat on the corner of her desk and enchanted us with the music of Sir Walter Scott's *Lady of the Lake*:

> *The stag at eve had drunk its fill,*
> *Where danced the moon on Monan's rill,*
> *And deep his midnight lair had made*
> *In lone Glenartney's hazel shade . . . .*

Later, as a teacher myself, I knew the delight of taking children into a great adventure with a story—the utter silence of the room, the intent look on the children's faces, and the involuntary sigh that escaped our lips at the conclusion of the episode. We had been together in the presence of good writing, and we felt bound together by the experience. My sojourn in that school was brief, but only recently a former student met me unexpectedly and eagerly told me what book she was reading. She could have paid me no greater compliment. Great literature has a way of building people. Books continue to be an influence far beyond my own words to these children.

What I am saying is simply this: As Christian parents we are concerned about building whole people—people who are alive emotionally, spiritually, intellectually. The instruction to *train up a child in the way he should go* encompasses so much more than teaching him the facts of the gospel. It is to train the child's character, to give him high ideals, and to encourage integrity. It is to provide largeness of thought, creative thinking, imaginative wondering—an adequate view of God and His world. He can never really appreciate the finest without personal redemption. But many a redeemed person lives in a small insecure world because he has never walked with God into the larger place which is His domain. We have books and the Book at our disposal to use wisely for God's glory.

A young child, a fresh uncluttered mind, a world before him—to what treasures will you lead him? With what will you furnish his spirit?

Pooh and Piglet nearly catch a Woozle.

2.

MILK AND HONEY

SOME TIME ago I borrowed a number of children's books from a friend whose family enjoys good books. When I returned them several days later, their three-year-old Jim welcomed back this familiar stack and carefully went through the books, his face lighting up with pleasure as he came upon favorites. Finally he found the special one he was looking for and hugged it to himself and said, "I *like* this one!" He was greeting an old friend.

He sat down to look through it, reciting the phrases which were dear to him, laughing at some pages, earnestly studying others. Even the size and the feel of the book seemed important to him—a prized possession.

Books are important to Jim because they are to his parents. He hears his mother and father talk about books at the dinner table, and they take time to read to him. Books are always treated with respect and care. None of the four children in this family have been permitted as babies to take old magazines and destroy the pages. It isn't proper respect for a book; books are handled with care and placed back on the shelf. In turn, each of the children have looked forward to the day when they could read and enter into the private, special world of books on their own.

Parents unconsciously teach their children what is valuable by the way they spend their own time. If television is more important to the parents than books, the children will likely choose the same. If the caliber of television and its advertising was consistently excellent, then perhaps less would be lost. Television is here to stay, and its better productions are highly recommended learning experiences. Certainly it would be folly for me in one paragraph to try to defeat the allurements of the screen. But families do have to repeatedly make conscious decisions about what is valuable and then choose the best over the mediocre. If appreciation of beauty and the gift of articulation are meaningful to you, then I suggest that exposure to great writing is a necessity.

The choice will sometimes be between a clean house with the television as morning baby-sitter or a partially clean house, no telephone conversations, and a half-hour of sharing a picture book. Or father might choose to delay the relaxation of reading his newspaper to make time for a story with the children.

A busy schedule is the enemy of reading. Agreeing in principle with all the benefits of books, you may at this point simply sigh and say, "I wish we had more time for reading." But the fact remains that we arrange time for what we think is truly important. Perhaps some other activities will have to be curtailed—committees, hobbies, clubs, church meetings, a wife's job—in order to free you to do what you decide is right to do.

A Swiss friend visiting in the States remarked about the telephone being the great intruder into American life. "Wherever I go," he said, "no matter how important a conversation, an activity, a meeting, or a peaceful dinner gathering, Americans willingly let the telephone interrupt whatever they are doing. It is as if they think God is calling!" An astute observation. We do let the telephone and the person on the other end of the line run our lives. We had the telephone company install a device on our telephone that enables us to turn the bell off. Important calls are dialed again later. For some things the world can wait!

I don't know anyone who would suggest that we follow each other like a herd of thoughtless animals, pushed about by life. We have freedom and capacity to choose. God's promise of wisdom to those who ask is given on the condition that the person open himself up to God's ideas and be ready to obey. I have a painful feeling that family life is often more obedient to a given sub-culture than to the Lord of glory. Each set of parents is charged with responsibility for their children. Each must choose goals which they deem valuable and then make private decisions to implement them. Life seems full of choices among good, better, and best. Only lazy parents avoid making decisions. And remember, parents bend the twig long before it gets to the schoolteacher.

The plea I am making is simply this—make time for books! Don't let your children live in spiritual poverty when abundance is available!

Erich Fromm in his book *The Art of Loving* speaks of a child's basic need for *milk* and *honey* from his parents. *Milk* is the symbol of the care a child receives for his physical needs, for his person. *Honey* symbolizes the sweetness of life, that special quality that gives the sparkle within a person. Fromm says, "Most mothers are capable of giving milk, but only a minority of giving honey, too." To give honey, one must love honey and have it to give. Good books are rich in honey.

In James Stephen's *The Crock of Gold*, a wise philosopher says, "I have learned . . . that the head does not hear anything until the heart has listened, and what the heart knows today the head will understand tomorrow." What a reservoir of wisdom good literature can store away for the heart!

What kind of books are proper fare for a child's mind? Discovering these will lift your own heart and give you a taste for honey. Once you begin enjoying good children's literature you will find yourself in a treasure house of reading. Take care in your new eagerness not to push your child into books beyond his years. While he may love them, it simply means he'll miss the books tailored just for his present years.

What kind of books? "Stories that make for wonder. Stories that make for laughter. Stories that stir one within with an understanding of the true nature of courage, of love, of beauty. Stories that make one tingle with high adventure, with daring, with grim determination, with the capacity of seeing danger through to the end. Stories that bring our minds to kneel in reverence; stories that show the tenderness of true mercy, the strength of loyalty, the unmawkish respect for what is good."[1] A good book is always an experience containing spiritual, emotional, and intellectual dimensions.

Picture books are a child's first introduction to the world of reading. He *reads* pictures. A little child expects the pictures to tell the story and to tell it accurately. Who can know all the impressions and data he stores up in his

---

[1]Ruth Sawyer, *The Way of the Storyteller* (New York: Viking Press, 1962), p. 157.

private world from a picture book? Such books provide the
fun of looking, but they also give an experience. By sharing their own observations, parents teach their children
how to look at pictures.

Some concept of art values will begin to form in the
child's mind as he looks at pictures. Don't take the illustrations in a book lightly. If a book which says good things
has illustrations which are stiff and stereotyped, use the
book anyway. You will be buying other books which contain really good illustrations as a child grows older. Expos-
ing him to a variety in art helps him to choose what he
likes. Make a point of commenting on colors and artistic
expression to help him see. The book listing in the appen-
dix designates outstanding illustrators.

However, a warning. Your view of art may not always be
a child's view of pleasing art. I'm thinking particularly
of some of the artwork done by illustrator Maurice Sendak, a favorite with children. Something of the child in
me responds to his hilarious drawings. But librarians
gasped in horror when Where the Wild Things Are was
chosen as a Caldecott Award winner. One children's librarian told me she was appalled and was certain children
would reject it. To her surprise there was a raid on every copy in the library. The book never stands idle on
the shelf.

Why did the children like it so much? Because Sendak
pictured what they would have drawn in the story of
rebellious Max and his adventure with the Wild Things.
Mr. Sendak has been deluged with drawings sent to him
by children, their own creations of Wild Things.

Ursula Nordstrom in an article in Saturday Review tells
of one four-year-old in a day-care center in Brooklyn who
would not speak except for an occasional indistinct utter-
ance. She was apathetic and unresponsive. Slow im-
provement began to appear in the storytelling time, and
when the teacher chose Where the Wild Things Are the

Snow is to roll in

Buttons are to
keep people warm

From *A Hole Is to Dig* by Ruth Krauss, illustrated by
Maurice Sendak. Copyright © 1952, as to text, by Ruth
Krauss. Copyright © 1952, as to pictures, by Maurice Sendak. Reprinted with permission of Harper & Row, Publishers.

child listened and looked intently. Afterward she approached the teacher and uttered her first sentence, "May I have that book?" Something in that book opened up a needy little girl, who has since become an avid lover of books and an affectionate child.

Many times children say, "Now I'll read you this story," and then proceed to read what the pictures are saying. Or, have you ever had your child say, "Don't read the writing, read the pictures." Begin to notice illustrators you and your children like and look for their work. (Incidentally, some artists change their style over a period of time. Mr. Sendak's more recent illustrations are not nearly as happy and light as his earlier ones.)

Kinds of Books

The best religious children's books are for younger boys and girls. When children become avid readers of adventure stories on their own, the distinctly religious market has far less quality to offer. Publishers have fussed over this problem, but I am not too disturbed because when we try too hard we end up with false concepts of sacred and secular. I believe God uses good children's books and therefore quality has high priority.

C. S. Lewis' children's books stand in a class apart for excellence. Paul White's *Jungle Doctor* books also affirm that Christian fiction can achieve a high standard, as do the books of Patricia St. John. (And don't forget the books of George MacDonald.) After these, the list of superior writers of what we call "Christian" fiction for children dwindles. The books I have mentioned are special, but general publishers of children's books have others that communicate values which are thoroughly Christian, if not overtly so. Generally it is better to acquaint your child with a book of quality than with second-rate writing where the plot is only a thin disguise for dumping the Christian message. Children have a precocious skill for skipping paragraphs, pages, and whole chapters if they feel a sermon coming, says Paul Hazard in his classic work on children's books.[2]

Every family should investigate the selection of complete Bible story books and choose one. Apart from these it is easy to recount only the more popular Bible stories instead of getting the sweep of Scripture.

The most important message we have to communicate to our children is about God, who He is and what He has done. He loves us, listens to us, and cares about our lives. If God is important to you, this will become a vital part of your sharing with your children, and you will use every helpful means to give instruction on this level.

But that's only the beginning. The whole world of things God made or let man discover is waiting for a child in books.

On our bookshelves stand twenty-three small volumes of the works of Beatrix Potter. The copyright dates are in the early 1900s, but I expect them to be as popular with our great-grandchildren as with our children. Her picture stories should be among the first owned by a child for his own personal library. Her illustrations are timeless, an inseparable part of her stories; her characterizations are brief, but ever so lucid. Your children simply must meet Peter Rabbit, Johnny Town Mouse, Squirrel Nutkin, Jemima Puddle Duck, Jeremy Fisher, and other unforgettable characters.

It was from Miss Potter that I first learned how much children love big words. Miss Potter's economy of words—she chooses just the right one while other authors might require many—gives liveliness to her stories, but every so often she tucks in a gem of a new word for children to roll over their tongues. The sparrows in *The Tale of Peter Rabbit* "implore him to exert himself" when

---

[2]Paul Hazard, *Books, Children and Men* (Boston, Mass.: Horn Books, 1960).

he is caught in a net by his jacket buttons. The gentleman fox in *The Tale of Jemima Puddle Duck* is "hospitable" and speaks of Jemima "commencing her tedious setting on the eggs," and Jemima herself complains of a "superfluous" hen who is too lazy to do so.

From *The Tale of Peter Rabbit* by Beatrix Potter, copyright © Frederick Warne & Co., Ltd. Used by permission.

Does this turn children off? No, seemingly not. I gathered my conclusions when I heard our own small child *implore* one of his friends to *exert himself*. Dr. Seuss makes the most of a child's fascination with words in his books, devising words out of his imagination that delight children, regardless of what adults think of them. Could it be that all words belong to children as much as to adults?

Families can grow together by discovering the fun of words. Happy is the home that has one parent at least who says, "Let's look it up!" and helps children to see that a dictionary is a fascinating friend. I remember the day "ubiquitous" occurred in something we read aloud together and with what pride that word became part of our household vocabulary.

Maybe you have wondered about the wisdom of fairy stories in your child's life I heard a man recently say that life wasn't really like Cinderella and that wicked step-mothers who want to kill beautiful daughters aren't the best fare for the mind. Others don't like elves and fairies and talking animals. Some refuse even Santa Claus.

You'll have to make up your own mind, but I, for one, like Cinderella and elves and talking animals and even Santa Claus. Children don't take life as seriously as adults and are more inclined to read for pleasure without theorizing until all the fun is wrung out. Fairy stories don't condone poor behavior; they simply relate what occurs. Children learn very early that there are good people, bad people, kind people, cruel people, and assortments of behavior in-between. And children have room in their lives for all sorts of miracles.

That's the problem, someone will say. If you let them believe in fairies and fantasy, how will they distinguish between truth and falsehood? I can't help thinking that since children love make-believe, they can easily tell the difference. At our house we have wondered if the silvery, dewy spider webs in the early morning sun had been part of the decorations for a ball the fairies held the night before, especially if some toadstools had sprung up in the same area. We discussed it as if it were true, but it was like sharing a special secret. We all knew it was make-believe. There is nothing unspiritual about an active imagination, a token of the liberty of childhood.

One of my young friends, at three, told me about the

tiger who lived in her backyard. I inquired about where
she kept him and what she fed him, and she told me the
details with great delight. Then I told her about the tiger
who lived in my backyard. Her eyes danced as I described
his strange behavior. Then she came very close and whis-
pered, "Is yours a real one?" When I said it wasn't, she said
confidentially, "Mine isn't either."

Was I encouraging her to lie? I think not. Both of us were
in on the world of pretend—a legitimate adventure. How
quickly we want to quench the fine spirit of childhood.
Imagination is the stuff out of which creativity comes, and
this little girl's artwork already shows a skillful amount of
this rare ingredient.

Our ten-year-old was in on a discussion with university
students traveling along in a car together. One student said
he would never tell his child about Santa Claus because
when he found out he wasn't real maybe the child would
conclude Jesus Christ wasn't real either. After listening to
the debate, our son came up with his contribution. "I knew
about Santa Claus, like I knew about elves and other pretend things. I never got him mixed up with the Lord Jesus
because I could tell from the way my parents talked and
acted all year long that Jesus was true."

If your experience has been different, perhaps we should
only conclude that there are a number of variables of
personality, emphasis, and other intangibles which might
make it so. C. S. Lewis once commented "that we who still
enjoy fairy tales have less reason to wish actual childhood
back. We have kept its pleasures and added some grown-
up ones as well."

A. A. Milne's Winnie the Pooh and The House at Pooh
Corner are examples of some of the finest kind of
fantasy—the kind which is ageless. One small child asked,
"Are you reading a children's book or am I reading a
grown-up book?" because that's the way Winnie the Pooh
is. It's full of talking animals with lovable personalities

and exceedingly humorous situations, for which age only increases appreciation.

Which brings us to the subject of humorous stories: a child's reading should be sprinkled with them. From the ludicrous situation of *Horton Hatches an Egg* to the more subtle humor and wisdom of *The Wind in the Willows* to the simpler boyish adventures of *Homer Price* and *Henry Huggins* or the magical girl named *Pippi Longstockings* who lived with a horse and a monkey—give your child large doses of these. Some nonsense is good for everyone, like the unforgettable tea party in *Alice in Wonderland*.

As children grow older they will enjoy tales of courage *(Call it Courage, The Matchlock Gun)*, stories about animals *(King of the Wind, Bambi,* a book which is usually read too young in a popularized version), adventure stories *(Caddie Woodlawn, Kon-Tiki),* and a wealth of experience in mysteries *(The Adventures of Sherlock Holmes, Adventures of Richard Hannay).* Biographies, epic hero tales, and historical novels are all part of rounding out the reading picture.

Children grow up hearing about classics, and some are conditioned against them because they feel that surely dullness and classic must go together. Sometimes this is because books we call classics are introduced poorly or too early. I prefer to call them "good books." They are classics because they have demonstrated the enduring qualities of good literature (discussed in chapter 3); therefore to cheapen or simplify them for popular reading is to end up with only a story, because the *classic* elements have either been deleted or diluted.

Some children like how-to-do-it or all-about-everything type books, but I suspect parents like them best because they look so educational. These really should be in a separate category because they don't usually classify as literature but are more nearly manuals of information. Paul Hazard suggests that instead of pouring out so much knowledge on a child's soul that it is crushed, we should plant a seed of an idea that will develop from inside. The most important knowledge is of the human heart, he concludes.

Should your child own books or just borrow them from a library? Probably some of each. Someone once said that a few well-chosen books all his own give a child a sense of value, companionship, and individuality and are more valuable than fifty volumes hastily read and returned to the library. Some books, which have stood the test of time and classify as outstanding literature, should be one's own. Yet, better to buy no book than to let price dictate a poor choice. Personally I would hate to limit any child's reading experience to what he could purchase when such wonderful libraries are available. On the other hand, we can use birthdays, Christmas, and special times to build a personal library.

Sometimes a parent comments, "Our older daughter loves books, but our second son seems to have no interest in reading at all."

Not all children take to books like ducks to puddles. Each child is a special person in his own way. Some are just poor readers and lack motivation. Reading comes hard for them. This is when family togetherness in books comes to the rescue, at least in part. Reading aloud and sharing a book demonstrates that stories are fun, that books are friends.

Getting children reading on their own might mean a careful curtailing of easier substitutes, but a parent in cooperation with a creative God ought to be able to come up with other assists. Try reading an exciting story together with such a child—a story one couldn't bear to leave uncompleted—and then push the child carefully out on his own. Make certain the project doesn't lead to failure because it is too difficult, and be available for help. Whetting his appetite this way and then helping him find another book by the same author could mean a fresh start for the child. But it takes a sensitive parent who cares. I am convinced that many poor readers have developed psychological blocks early in their reading career, often by comparing themselves with rapid readers who leave them behind in the dust.

Don't put a premium on speed, and never say, "That book is much too young for you!" If he can read it, let him. (Make sure he doesn't have a schoolteacher who is belittling him this way.) Coax him onward without threatening his self-image in the complicated joy of reading.

Honey is a special treat, not a medicinal treatment.

> *Happy, happy it is to be*
> *Where the greenwood hangs o'er the dark blue sea;*
> *To roam in the moonbeams clear and still*
> *And dance with the elves*
> *Over dale and hill;*
> *To taste their cups, and with them roam*
> *The fields for dewdrops and honeycomb.*[3]

---

[3]Walter de la Mare, "Ann and the Fairy Song."

3.

WHAT MAKES A GOOD BOOK

GOOD BOOKS are written not so much *for* children as written *by* people who have not lost their childhood. Since men are really only grown-up children, good books appeal to all ages. C. S. Lewis said that no book is really worth reading at the age of ten which is not equally worth reading at the age of fifty. Children's books cannot be written *for* or down *to* children. They reject books which do not treat them as equals. The "My dear little reader" approach never really pleased children.

When men first began printing books, no one thought of books for children. Only dull, moralistic books were foisted on children by adults. Hans Christian Andersen was unique in his contribution to children and his capacity for being a grown-up child. In many ways he turned the tide in children's literature, and adults were even more surprised by the way children appropriated Daniel Defoe's *Robinson Crusoe* for their very own, capturing every boy's dream of adventure.

Real books have life. They release something creative in the minds of those who absorb them. The author captures reality, the permanent stuff of life, and something is aroused in the heart of the reader that endures.

A good book has a profound kind of morality—not a cheap, sentimental sort which thrives on shallow plots and superficial heroes, but the sort of force which inspires the reader's inner life and draws out all that is noble. A good writer has something worthy to say and says it in the best possible way. Then he respects the child's ability to understand. Principles are not preached but are implicit in the writing.

Walter de la Mare said, "I know well that only the rarest kind of best in anything is good enough for the young."[1] Childhood is so brief and yet so open and formative. Impressions are taken into maturity. I cannot believe that children exposed to the best of literature will later choose that which is cheap and demeaning. That is why only the best is good enough for children, for we are shaping a future.

Of the writing of children's books today there is no end, but many of these have no claim as literature. The publishing of children's books is a profitable enterprise in our affluent society, and the market is deluged with what may appear on the surface to be everything a child needs. I'm not sure it is laziness that lets parents buy these; I think it is more a lack of exposure to what is truly good in children's literature.

We have already discussed simplified classics. Included

---

[1]Walter de la Mare, *Bells and Grass* (New York: Viking).

in my bibliography are only two. One is *Little Pilgrim's Progress*, which in depth of writing in no way approximates the style of John Bunyan. *Pilgrim's Progress* as originally written by Bunyan is if anything more readable than the King James Bible. The marvelous imagery of this great book is couched in Bunyan's excellent prose. If you are among the families who choose the original, you will then have read Bunyan. But I am a realist. To miss any experience at all of the spiritual exercise and imagery of *Pilgrim's Progress* seems too great a loss to me, so I have included the simplified. The literary heart of the book is missing, but the ideas are there. Your children will be caught up in the wonder of Christian's journey and be exposed to great truths. The second is a very well-done *Tales from Shakespeare*, which hopefully will prepare the reader to enjoy Shakespeare at a later date.

The Disney-style versions of stories do children no favors. They are never as good as the original. Don't buy diluted editions. Pamela Travers' *Mary Poppins* in its original form must be read if you will know Mary Poppins. And Tom Sawyer must be met in a book, no matter how well the television version is received. I cajoled our son into reading Twain, and he had no embarrassment in thanking me. He remarked, "What the words help you to see and feel inside is much better than television!"

Which is precisely the problem with television; it can kill personal creativity. We don't even have to wonder what the characters look like. And while a good actor can portray intense emotion, it brings to the viewer a different experience than words do. And it cheats us of the opportunity to learn how to express what we feel in words.

But we still haven't answered the heart of the question. What makes one book superior and another inferior? Let's begin by taking apart the elements of a book. First, we

"Mary Poppins," they cried.
"Mary Poppins, come back!"

begin with the idea behind the book. What is the author trying to say? We call this the theme, and a weak theme results in a flabby story.

To get across the theme, the writer must use words, language. How the author uses language is called style. Every writer forms his sentences differently and thus weaves his personality into his writing. Word choices reveal the author's skill because they carry action, emotion, truth—and make the music of good prose.

Plot is the design of the idea. Good plots grow out of strong themes. Plot doesn't answer "What happened next?" Plot answers "Why?" The plot holds the story together in such a way that events take on meaning. Involved in plot is characterization. The skill with which the author makes the characters memorable and makes them live for us determines in large measure the quality of the story. What a difference between the characters of Robert Louis Stevenson's *Treasure Island* and a story where the characters are like puppets on a string, enabling the reader to outguess the author. Who can forget Long John Silver, the pirate of pirates? Terrifying, yet somehow likeable; cruel, yet somehow kind; he is no stereotyped, one-handed character. If Stevenson had less artistry in defining his characters and plot, a wildly unrealistic piece of writing would have resulted, and we would have long since forgotten Long John Silver.

What a convincing person Mary Poppins is! How unforgettable is Frodo of the Hobbit books or Toad of Toad Hall. Children can't define what charms them, but give them the right thing and they recognize it. They will have little use for stories which are shallow, insipid, awkward, labored, and overly moralistic.

Letters come every day to Harper & Row addressed to Laura Ingalls Wilder, author of *Little House on the Prairie* and others. Long since dead, Laura is still alive to these children. One child wrote, "Oh, Laura, if I was you I would have kicked Nellie Oleson in the leg when she was mean to you!"

Another mother told the Harper's Children's Book Editor that when they moved to a more spacious apartment with a guest room, her son had asked eagerly, "Now can Mr. White come and stay overnight with us?" He loved the author because he had given him the joy of *Charlotte's Web*. A young friend of ours sent one of her stories to C. S. Lewis asking for his critique and inquiring into his method for plotting stories. Because he was C. S. Lewis, he answered her as seriously as he would have answered a letter from an important man of letters. Children *do* know. Only this summer, a ten-year-old sighed, "I wish Mr. Lewis had not died. I'd like more of his kind of stories."

The quality of the idea, the skill of the plot, the depth of the characterization, the distinctive style of the author—that's the best I can do by way of defining a good book.

No one has yet sat down and devised a set of rules that magically produces a great story. The quality that we have talked about has to come from the quality inside the person writing the story. In 1945 Jesse Jackson wrote *Call Me Charley*, the story of the only black boy in a white school. Mr. Jackson did not set out to deliver a message on race relations. He simply wrote a book out of his own experience. It had the ring of reality, and twenty years later the book's editor would hear a woman tell how she had read a book in the fifth grade that changed her life, her whole attitude about people. The book was *Call Me Charley*.

That which is excellent has a certain spirit of literature present. The sensitivity of the reader says, "This is true." "This is real." And it sets in action something in the reader which profoundly affects him. It has been an experience—spiritual, imaginative, intellectual, or social. A sense of permanent worthwhileness surrounds really great literature. Laughter, pain, hunger, satisfaction, love, joy—the ingredients of human life are found in depth and leave a residue of mental and spiritual richness in the reader.

If we familiarize our children with this kind of writing, then they have a ground for making comparisons. Not everything they read will be excellent, but they will know a story's possibilities. It will set their reading patterns in motion.

I have already mentioned the importance of illustrations. A great variety of styles should be part of a child's inheritance, not just the parent's current preference. Bright colors, gentle pastels, bold strokes, whimsical lines, quaint old-fashioned pictures, modern design, pen and ink sketches—the story will demand a certain mood for the child. Some of you may not like the illustrators I have noted, but over the years children have chosen them as favorites.

Some books simply look more readable than others. White space, style of type, and paper quality may decide what is acceptable. That is to say, a good book should look like a good book!

Have you ever noticed how children look for a book in the library? They stare at the bindings, reading the titles. So many books, so many shelves—how does one choose? A few children whose parents have taught them which authors to look for or how to choose a book may invade the library with the confidence of a vacuum cleaner, scooping up everything good in sight. But for most this is not true. Parents know what I mean, because without some help, they feel a similar bewilderment. The librarian is often otherwise involved and not available for help. I know so well the anguish of a child who asks, "Teacher, could you help me find a good book?" Knowing about good books requires some learning time.

That's why I have written this book. The bibliography does not contain all the good books available, but it is a

Wilbur blushed, "But I'm not terrific,
Charlotte. I'm just average for a pig."

beginning. These have stood the test of time and/or of children's choice. Notice authors' names and teach your children to do likewise. It's the secret to conquering library-fear. If your child enjoys one of Kate Seredy's books (and I hope she does!), then she will doubtless want to read others by this author. Experience is the best teacher.

Don't make the mistake of saying, "Here is a book you must read." A child may decide without opening the cover that this is just the book he does *not* want to read. Don't force any book. Make excursions to the library a learning time for you and the children. Better to say, "This book looks like fun." or "Here's one you might enjoy." or "What do you think of this book?"

In our family we recommend books to each other regularly and take opinions seriously. It's lonely not to have someone else share a book which has touched you in some way. Family closeness is not suddenly developed when children reach a certain age; it must begin from the first. A special joy comes when you hear your small child say to you, "You'll love it," as he recommends Lois Lenski's *Little Train*.

One of my favorite memories involves just such a time of sharing a book. Traveling abroad we had purchased Elizabeth Goudge's *The Little White Horse* for our twelve-year-old son to read. He enjoyed it so much he repeatedly said, "Mom, you've just got to read this book." One night I stayed back from an art lecture in Florence, Italy, which I had hoped to attend and spent the evening with him instead. I read *that* book. I was as delighted as he, and commented on incidents as I read. He was absorbed in his own book, but suddenly came over to my chair, gave me a tight hug, and said spontaneously, "I just had to tell you this minute I loved you!" I was taking time to enjoy *his* book. I treasure that evening. No art lecture could have done for us what sharing that book did, and later father read it aloud to us again.

One of the teachers in our city read Roald Dahl's *Charlie and the Chocolate Factory* to her class. They must have shared the fun of the book on the playground because seemingly half of the school came into the library to ask for the book. The librarian got the idea finally and ordered several copies. She said to me, "It isn't on *any* list, but I can't keep a copy on the shelves." Which all goes to show that children will like what they will, and I suspect that's how books get on lists.

Every child in your family may not like every book in this bibliography. That would be expecting far too much. You may ask, "Why didn't she put this book on her list? We loved it." There wasn't room for them all. Keep it on your list and share the title with others. The bibliography has this caption, *Books Children Should Have the Opportunity to Enjoy*. Expose them to the variety, read some of the books aloud, but let the children ultimately decide what they enjoy.

You will notice some books are labeled Caldecott or Newbery Award winners. Librarians tell me that some parents come in and, without any reference to the child's interest say, "I'd like a Caldecott book." The 1967 Newbery Award winner illustrates the folly of this. Irene Hunt's *Up a Road Slowly* is a beautifully written story for a teen-age girl who is by nature reflective and serious. Saying, "This is good literature" will probably not make a carefree tomboy like it. Wisdom demands that as parents we make some effort to understand both books and children.

Boys and girls go through a stage, usually around ten years of age, where they consume series books. Christian and secular publishers have numerous adventure series. For some it will be the *Sugar Creek Gang* series; for others it will be the *Tarzan* series. The *Twin* books by Lucy Fitch Perkins are also quite popular. No books in my bibliography fall into this classification, but that is not because they are harmful. In general, they just do not classify as superior literature but seem to meet a need in a child's life. While waiting for this stage to pass, I'd be ready to recommend some others at the right moment.

Good literature teaches more than we know. Example always speaks louder than precept, and books can do more to inspire honor and tenacity of purpose than all the scoldings and exhortations in the world.

The teaching is accumulative, too. The other day our high schooler was discussing two destructive children. He said, "I got to thinking about how I would teach my children not to pull up wild flowers by the roots and destroy things, and then I wondered how I had learned myself. I decided I had learned from books to respect the world. In C. S. Lewis's books the animals and trees have personality; in pioneer stories Indians tried to walk through the forest without breaking a twig, and settlers respected the land; in Tolkien's books, the orcs are the bad guys who leave a path of careless destruction." He concluded, "You put a whole childhood of reading together, and you don't have to take a conservation course."

From *The Book of Giant Stories* by David L. Harrison,
illustrated by Philippe Fix. Copyright © 1972 by Philippe
Fix. Used with permission of McGraw-Hill Book Company.

4.

FANTASY AND REALISM

ALICE FOUND herself falling mile after mile down the Rabbit's Hole until she thought she might be near the center of the earth. Presently she began to wonder if she would fall right through the earth.

"Well," thought Alice to herself, "after such a fall as this, I shall think nothing of tumbling down stairs."

Fantasy is like that. It makes "tumbling down stairs" relatively harmless. The very disparity between this magical world and ours somehow puts personal problems in perspective. I don't know quite how, but life seems more manageable and humankind more courageous after reading fantasy.

Well-written fantasy grabs the reader and gets him in-

51

volved because it is, first of all, the simple pleasure of a good story. One meets characters of substance, like A. A. Milne's Winnie-the-Pooh with his honey and good humor, or the resourceful Mary Poppins, full of surprises, or the noble and courageous Frodo of *The Lord of the Rings.* The events of a fantasy are skillfully woven to create suspense and round the story off to a proper climax. Good fantasy meets the criteria of all good literature.

But there is more to good fantasy than that. It demands something extra of its readers; it asks them to pay attention. If one listens carefully, a second level of meaning soon become obvious, and that, combined with the simple pleasure of a good story, makes the book worth reading over and over—worth reading at age ten and worth reading at fifty!

Some people object and say all those hidden meanings are lost on children. Lewis Mumford once said, "The words are for children, and the meanings are for men." But I don't believe it. Children suspect more is present than the actual story, and because there is little space between the real and the unreal world in a child's mind, they reach across with amazing ease and begin to ferret it out. They may read the story again years later and find that their experiences- in life help them see more. Adults will read the same book and begin to better understand why they loved it as children. But at any age, the story is an experience of quality and substance.

The most subtle and profound ideas are often found in books written for children. A kind of "suspended reality" exists in which what is true becomes more obvious. Good fantasy helps us see "reality in unreality, credibility in incredibility." A child accepts and loves fantasy because of his own rich imagination and sense of wonder. For children, magical things are not nearly as complicated as they are for adults. They have room in their minds for all sorts of happenings. And those who write fantasy are not so much those who understand the heart of a child as those who have a child's heart themselves. Out of the depth of their personal experience they combine a child's heart with profound insights into life's meaning. Some fantasies laugh; some are full of nonsense; others are breathless with adventure and brave deeds. If you listen, you will hear more than the obvious story line.

For instance, back to the ridiculous events of *Alice in Wonderland*. The White Queen says, "The rule is, jam to-morrow, and jam yesterday—but never jam today."

"It *must* come sometimes to 'jam today,'" Alice objected.

"No, it can't," said the Queen. "It's jam every *other* day: to-day isn't any *other* day, you know."

"I don't understand you," said Alice. "It's dreadfully confusing."

But the reader is somehow amused, not confused. He appreciates the fantastic logic of the queen just as he understands Alice's matter-of-fact mind. Because life is sometimes like that. The language in the story is the language of nonsense, but at the same time there is an essence of truth contained in it. Perhaps that is why allusions to *Alice* are used again and again in literature and conversations. As the Red Queen said to Alice, "Even a joke should have some meaning."

Not everyone takes to fantasies or fairy tales, although I believe most children do. These stories are certainly at their best when read aloud—especially fairy stories —because the lovely cadence of words and the economy of language make them a special experience. It is adults who worry over the make-believe, the magic, the strange creatures, the evil events, the wars, and sometimes the gore. Children have far less trouble. They readily know the difference between fantasy and reality. "No child confuses dragons or unicorns with cattle in a meadow," one writer said. It is the child who doesn't know about dragons and unicorns who is to be pitied!

I've never met a child (although there may be one) who has analyzed the emotional and physical impropriety of nursery rhymes like

> There I met an old man
> Who would not say his prayers,
> I took him by the left leg
> And threw him down the stairs.

That's simply a ludicrous scene and a good rhyme. Children don't squeeze life into boxes. They have room for a large variety of emotions and happenings and are quite aware of the possibilities in people. They know life is difficult; they are happy to believe it also turns out right in the end. I like *Beauty and the Beast* to this day because in that tale an act of love transforms what is ugly into something beautiful. I believe it still happens.

Bruno Bettelheim, one of the world's leading child psychologists, contends that fairy tales provide children with an invaluable education in good and evil. He believes that every child has a rich supply of personal fantasies filled with fears and anxieties and that fairy tales reassure him and offer solutions. He learns how to deal constructively with his fears. Happy endings tell him that solutions and hope are real and model the kind of happy life the child wants to find. "Like all great art, fairy tales both delight and instruct; their special genius is that they do so in terms which speak directly to children."[1] Fairy tales, says Bettelheim, help children (and adults) answer such questions as: What is the world really like? How am I to live my life in it? How can I be myself?

While these metaphysical questions are handled in fairy tales and fantasies, they suggest rather than dictate answers. A good fantasy is not a thinly disguised moral

[1]Bruno Bettelheim,*The Uses of Enchantment: The Meaning and Importance of Fairy Tales* (New York: Alfred A. Knopf, 1976), p. 53.

message; it asks profound questions that develop out of the plot and the characters of the story. The word *fantasy* comes from the Greek and literally translated means *a making visible*. A proper story makes visible certain basic realities; it demonstrates options in handling life's situations.

For instance, sometimes we falter in the face of evil. We tell ourselves that we don't have all the information, and we excuse our personal indecision. Then we read a story and something inside us says *yes, this is how we are to act*. "How shall a man judge what to do in such times?" asks a character in *The Lord of the Rings*. "As he ever has judged," comes the reply. "Good and evil have not changed. . . . It is man's part to discern them."

Our favorite fantasies are written by George MacDonald, C. S. Lewis, J. R. R. Tolkien, and Charles Williams. (One wonders why the English are so much better at this kind of writing than Americans.) We have read C. S. Lewis's *Narnia Chronicles* (and his space trilogy) more often than any others. He offers us a vivid story filled with extraordinary events and familiar details. He expands our world with his view of loyalty, his differing concept of time, his logic, his view of truth, love, evil, and goodness—and the wonder of the imagination.

In a scene from *The Magician's Nephew* Lewis's characters explore dimensions of love and temptation and loyalty. Aslan, the golden-maned Lion (who is no ordinary lion), sends Digory and Polly, two children, to a faraway garden to get an apple to plant in the land of Narnia as a tree of protection. When they finally arrive at the place and Digory gets into the garden to pick the golden apple, he is confronted by a witch. She tells him that the apple gives youth and health to whoever eats it, and she encourages him to take one for himself and eat it. He is hungry, isn't he? Digory refuses, but he does remember his mother who is dying, and the witch urges him to take the apple to her.

Aslan need never know. "Soon she will be quite well again. All will be well again. Your home will be happy again." Digory gasps as if he has been hurt and puts his hand to his head, for he knows that the most terrible choice lies before him. The witch also suggests he leave Polly behind. At once all that the witch has been saying to him sounds false and hollow. He remembers the shining tears in Aslan's eyes and the promise he had made to Aslan. He returns to Narnia and walks straight up to Aslan, hands him the apple, and says, "I've brought you the apple you wanted, sir." "Well done," says Aslan in a voice that makes the earth shake.

Suddenly anything other than obedience and loyalty seems incredibly stupid. We have never read this story without feeling a profound longing to keep our promises and to do what is right—not because we have heard a sermon but because of the action and decisions of the characters in the story. I am convinced that fantasies quicken the ability to extract and apply principles in life as readers learn to make a transfer of ideas from allegory to reality. Good literature should always make life larger.

And fantasy is not just for children. Some who have not grown old on the inside have always reveled in it; others have found their way into it as adults, maybe to escape a harsh world. *Watership Down* met with tremendous response from adults and has been quickly appropriated by children. (Over a hundred years ago the same thing happened with a different kind of allegory: John Bunyan's *Pilgrim's Progress*.) Though hardly comparable in quality, *Jonathan Livingston Seagull* had phenomenal sales and found its way into homes all over America. Adults reveled in it; children disdained it. They were quick to see that there was little substance or depth to the story. What it said was not true.

At the same time, adults began to push realism onto children. Editors, convinced that children needed "rele-

From *The Biggest Bear* by Lynd Ward. Copyright © 1952.
Reproduced by permission of Houghton Mifflin Company.

vant books," began to spew these books into the marketplace. Salesmen convinced bookstore buyers; librarians, eager to be contemporary, recommended them for reading. Someone once said that the worst features of an era are accented in the children's books of that period. A crusading, awareness era has dumped all our societal problems into children's books. Children's reading lists now include categories on divorce, physical handicaps, old age and death, minority problems, poverty, inner city life, ecology, war, magic and astrology, and others. In some cases it is not the subject I disagree with so much as the way the subject is handled. These are books with a message, often with inconsequential plots and characters, thinly disguised "moralisms" which editors have so disdained in a more puritanical age. Except that the books in question are hardly puritanical. Their "moralisms" derive from the contemporary emphasis that we must all be understanding and non-condemning. In doing this, I believe they demean human potential.

The treatment of some subjects is explicit, vulgar, and inappropriate. Inane incidents are added to the story to make it "spicy," often harmless enough in one sense, yet adding nothing to the story or to the depth of characterization. It's almost a plot to spoil childhood! One editor defended these books, saying they are obviously meeting the needs of young people because of their popularity. That is the same argument used in favor of pornographic magazines.

Personally, I think it is an outrageous hoax to pawn these off on the young, and no book editor is going to convince me that these books bring anything lasting or good to a child. All they bring is a depressing point of view. A good book inspires the inner person with hope for the future. Books that do not stir a child's imagination are a waste of time.

We are burdening children with minority problems,

poverty, world hunger, pollution, and broken families. Anne Carroll Moore describes these as "lifeless stories with too much background and too many problems." One young girl commented, "Oh, those gray books. I don't like them." I don't like them either, and I believe parents ought to be sure enough of themselves to resist such trends. Reading lists are sometimes influenced by a few powerful New York editorial decisions. This issue has become the great debate in children's literature.

I see stores marketing even something as seemingly innocent as Silverstein's *The Giving Tree* and see eager grandparents buying it for their grandchildren, and I want to tell them, "That's not a children's book. That's an adult's idea of what children should like." It offers no possibilities to a child; it contains no substance. People talk about its great symbolism, and I say, "Bosh! It's a waste of time."

Authors of books for upper elementary and early teen readers are now treating dope, alcohol, sexual problems, and rape in their stories, using formerly taboo words and even homosexual characters. Defenders of these books believe there is a need for candor because so many children feel isolated in their real-life situations. Surely, they say, a young person reading stories about parents with excessive drinking problems would be comforted to know others share his problems. For readers with no such experience, it gives understanding and compassion for others.

On the surface that sounds convincing. Compassion and understanding are the by-products of good reading, and I'm heartily in favor of children having wider worlds than their own. All good reading should accomplish this. But many of these new books are faddish, exploiting the permissiveness of our age, and will not stand the test of time or of good literature. Do they illumine in significant ways what is true? Mr. Micawber in Dicken's *David Copperfield* is no paragon of virtue. Why are his character and the details of his life so memorable? Can the reader understand or sympathize with the incredible complexities of Micawber's family life that resulted from his indiscretions? Mr. Micawber, Little Emily, and Uriah Heep are even somewhat shocking if you describe them out of context. Good literature *does* deal with reality, but not in the burdened way of contemporary writers.

Somehow there's a vast difference between a novel like *David Copperfield*, or even the famous *Upstairs, Downstairs* series on public television, and the afternoon soap operas. The themes are not at fault, but the way they are treated somehow debases human experience. Reality fairy tales are *not* morally superior to fantasy fairy tales.

Paula Fox, author of *Portrait of Ivan*, writes:

> We offer sentimentalized information about copulation, tricked out with patronizing argot, as insulting to young readers as those "youth" movies ground out by aging film-makers whose purpose, one knows, is not only high-minded but also passionately financial. At last we are letting the ignorant child in on the secret.
> Yet the real secret we keep to ourselves because we lack the courage and imagination to say it. It is the knowledge of what it is to be human, the knowledge that we are human from the first second we leap into the world and wail out our first breath. But that secret can only be revealed by the eternal mystery of the imagination, which works gaily with the most terrible truths. [2]

A good book is not problem-centered; it is people-centered. It reveals how to be a human being and what the possibilities of life are; it offers hope.

Somehow, lacking a more imaginative way to cope with life, adults throw the weight of the world's problems back on the young. Instead of having students read the classics (books that have stood the test of time), high school

---

[2]Paula Fox, "Bitter-Coated Sugar Pills," *Saturday Review*, 19 September 1970.

teachers weight book lists with faddish contemporary writing, often full of hate and fear. We may not change a teacher's book list, but we can encourage the right fare at home. Given a book of imagination and hope, I don't believe children will choose less, except in an effort to please.

Some time ago a bookstore buyer enthusiastically showed me a stack of the "new books." One pleased the eye with exceptionally lovely watercolor illustrations and a simple story line (at an outrageous price). It was a picture book for young children about a bird looking for a place to nest, each year finding more and more pollution, and finally flying off "the last free bird on earth." Why would any adult perpetrate that kind of hopelessness on a little child? The other books in the stack were simply messages about war, famine, and other discouraging topics, books bent on taking the spirit out of a child. My guess is that those books, so interesting to some adults, were rejected by children.

Give me and my children a well-written story that "reiterates the old verities that kindness and goodness will triumph over evil if they are backed by wisdom, wit and courage. These are basic truths we should like built into the depth of the child's consciousness."[3]

Only two kinds of books have been mentioned in this chapter—fantasy and the new trend in realism. Your children will want a wider variety than fantasy—fiction, non-fiction, historical fiction, information books, poetry. A good reading list like the bibliography at the back of this book will help you choose. You will also find on the list sensitively written books about handicaps (The Door in the Wall, Mine for Keeps, The Summer of the Swans), many books whose characters are from minority groups, books about being poor (Evan's Corner, Blue Willow, The

---

[3]May Hill Arbuthnot, Children and Books (Glenview, Ill.: Scott, Foresman and Company, 1964).

Hundred Dresses, Judy's Journey), books about ecology (*The Seal and the Slick*), and others. At first glance, some of these may appear to be "problem" books, but I believe for the most part they are more than that and will stand the test of time. My point is that these themes are not new in literature. Good literature has always dealt with truth, but not in a way that makes man less. Good literature shows man how to be more.

5.

POETRY

What is Poetry? Who knows?
Not the rose, but the scent of the rose;
Not the sky, but the light in the sky;
Not the fly, but the gleam of the fly;
Not the sea, but the sound of the sea;
Not myself, but what makes me
See, hear and feel something that prose
Cannot: and what it is, who knows![1]

POETRY IS a kind of verbal music. It is more than just doggerel that rhymes. It appeals more to feelings than to intellect. In poetry we get the shape and feel of words. Children may learn to appreciate poetry more than adults do because they are free to let it be what it is and not demand more of it.

---

[1]Eleanor Farjeon, *Poems for Children* (Philadelphia, Pa.: Lippincott, 1951).

From *Granfa' Grig Had a Pig* by Wallace Tripp. Illustrations copyright © 1976 by Wallace Tripp. Reproduced by permission of Little, Brown and Co.

Children first meet poetry in the repetitious rhythm of nursery rhymes. Most of them are nonsensical:
"A pocketful of rye, four and twenty blackbirds baked in a pie. . . ." (What a feathery idea!)
"Jack and Jill went up the hill to fetch a pail of water. . . ." (Strange place to find a well!)
But the sense really doesn't matter. In fact, I must confess that some poems which come most frequently to my mind are nonsensical ones from happy childhood memories. Their beat and verbal song seem to stick. That's why children often say when hearing nursery rhymes read, "Sing it again."

I have in my notebook an interesting quote that bears on the subject. Whether it came from a conversation or a famous writer, I have long since forgotten, but it is worth sharing. "Do you know what is wrong with people who never read nursery rhymes? I will tell you. When little boys and girls grow bigger and older, they should grow from the outside, leaving a little boy in the middle; even when they are quite grown up, the little child that once they were should be within them. But some unlucky people grow older from inside and so grow old through and through." That has always seemed a dreadful fate to me.

The first poetry books used at our house included Milne's *When We Were Very Young* and *Now We Are Six*. The poems vary from the nonsensical and eccentric to the warm and familiar. The contribution of Ernest Shepard's excellent illustrations add much to our enjoyment of these poems. Here are some excerpts:

> They're changing the guard at Buckingham
>   Palace—
> Christopher Robin went down with Alice.
> Alice is marrying one of the guard,
> "A soldier's life is terrible hard,"
>   Says Alice.

or,

> Ernest was an elephant, a great big fellow
> Leonard was a lion with a six foot tail,
> George was a goat, and his beard was yellow,
> And James was a very small snail.

From an appealing cadence such as this, what would
you naturally name a lion or a goat at your house?

Have you ever loved to chant this one while taking a
walk?

> Whenever I walk in a London street,
> I'm ever so careful to watch my feet,
> And I keep in the squares
> And the masses of bears
> Who wait at the corners all ready to eat
> The sillies who tread on the lines of the street,
> Go back to their lairs
> And I say to them, "Bears,
> Just look how I'm walking in all of the squares!"

By all means give children generous doses of A. A.
Milne, Edward Lear, and Hilaire Belloc—just for fun.

Reading poetry is not the same as reading a story. Listening to poetry, a child becomes accustomed to words in an
unfamiliar arrangement and to the cadence of the meter.
Words "rise and fall and flow and pause and echo—like
the singing of birds at daybreak or a little before the fall of
night when daffodils 'take the winds of March with
beauty.'"[2]

Poetry is like music in that it has to have sound to be
appreciated. Reading poetry aloud to a receptive child is
one of the rewards of parenthood. The surprise and beauty
of words may break on a child like the dawning of a fresh
world, and he will be forever a lover of poetry.

Poems, like good seasonings, should be sprinkled
lightly on the life of a child. One here, another delightful

---

[2]Walter de la Mare, Tom Tiddler's Ground (New York: Knopf, 1962).

There was an Old Man on
  whose nose
Most birds of the
  air could repose;
But they all flew away at the closing of day,
Which relieved that Old Man and his nose.

From *The Complete Nonsense Book* by Edward Lear. Reprinted with permission of Dodd, Mead & Company.

one there. Too much deadens the ability to hear and helps some children decide that poetry is wearisome. Boys and girls usually have a natural ear for poetry and a great capacity for enjoyment if the development of this kind of reading keeps pace with growth in other areas.

Lewis Gannett, who compiled *The Family Book of Verse*, writes, "When I was small, my father read poetry to the family at breakfast each morning, and on Sunday afternoons he read longer poetry to those who came to listen. I seem to recall sometimes resenting the morning delay before eating . . . yet, rereading old poems . . . again and again I seem to be hearing—and appreciating—echoes of my father's voice. I observe that my daughter reads every night—sometimes poetry—to her six daughters and they obviously enjoy it. It would be a proud boast if this book should help encourage the old custom of reading poetry aloud at home."

I include Gannett's comments for obvious reasons. Your children may not coax you to read a poem. Sometimes when you are bent upon sharing one, they may give you a look of patient endurance. But valuable experiences are not always appreciated at the time; later they yield their rewards. We do many things for our families because we decide they are right to do. The spirit, the attitude, the sense of adventure with which they are done makes all the difference! And I have often seen in our house a warm look of love that says secretly, "My father is special!" when my husband reads a poem, introducing it with, "My dad used to read this to us. . . ."

Of course, you'll want to read some from Robert Louis Stevenson's *A Child's Garden of Verses* for warmth of childhood pleasures.

> *A birdie with a yellow bill*
> *Hopped upon the window sill.*
> *Cocked his shining eye and said,*
> *"Ain't you 'shamed, you sleepy-head?"*

Or do you remember:

> I saw you toss the kites on high
> And blow the birds about the sky;
> And all around I heard you pass
> Like ladies' skirts across the grass—
> O wind, a-blowing all day long,
> O wind, that sings so loud a song!

Eleanor Farjeon's poetry for children has a wit and melody all its own. Sounds and senses are accentuated in the poetry of Carl Sandburg and Robert Frost. Here is Frost's "The Pasture":

> I'm going out to clean the pasture spring;
> I'll only stop to rake the leaves away
> (And wait to watch the water clear, I may):
> I sha'n't be gone long—You come too.
> I'm going out to fetch the little calf
> That's standing by the mother. It's so young,
> It totters when she licks it with her tongue.
> I sha'n't be gone long—You come too.

Feel Carl Sandburg's "Fog":

> The fog comes
> on little cat feet.
> It sits looking
> over harbor and city
> on silent haunches
> and then moves on.

Sara Teasdale and Christina Rossetti often wrote about nature. Children feel in their hearts what Sara Teasdale shared in this excerpt from "Barter":

> Life has loveliness to sell—
> All beautiful and splendid things,
> Blue waves whitened on a cliff,
> Climbing fire that sways and sings,
> And children's faces looking up
> Holding wonder like a cup.

Each poet brings his own style, his own emotional

wealth to the poem. Anthologies give us the best opportunity to sample many flavors of poetry. Several of these are listed in the bibliography.

When you are first introducing poetry to a child; you will use happy verse—nonsensical, exaggerated, cozy—whatever you choose. As the child grows older, don't shy away from poetry which you may think is too deep or too sad for him. Trust the child to understand more than he can express. He may or may not say to you, "That poem understands me," but that may be what he feels inside. For instance, listen to the mood of Edna St. Vincent Millay's "God's World":

> O world, I cannot hold thee close enough!
>   Thy winds, thy wide gray skies!
>   Thy mists that roll and rise!
> Thy woods, this autumn day, that ache and sag
> And all but cry with color!

Or Emily Dickinson's "Have You Got a Brook?"

> Have you got a brook in your little heart,
> Where bashful flowers blow,
> And blushing birds go down to drink
> And shadows tremble so?
>
> And nobody knows, so still it flows,
> That any brook is there;
> And yet your little draught of life
> Is daily drunken there.

By all means, share old favorites like Longfellow's "Paul Revere's Ride":

> Listen, my children, and you shall hear
> Of the midnight ride of Paul Revere,
> On the eighteenth of April, in Seventy-five;
> Hardly a man is now alive
> Who remembers that famous day and year.

Or the romance of Alfred Noyes' "The Highwayman":

> The wind was a torrent of darkness among
>   the gusty trees,

The moon was a ghostly galleon tossed upon
  cloudy seas,
The road was a ribbon of moonlight over the
  purple moor,
    And the highwayman came riding—
      Riding—riding—
The highwayman came riding, up to the old
  inn door.

Samuel Taylor Coleridge's "The Rime of the Ancient Mariner" will stir the heart of a child who is entering his teens. Don't you remember the thirsty feeling of this haunting tale?

Water, water everywhere,
And all the boards did shrink;
Water, water everywhere,
Nor any drop to drink

Or read his "Christabel" and "Kubla Khan," so rich in imagination. The list extends endlessly, for there are so many to be met and enjoyed—William Blake, E. E. Cummings, John Donne, Kipling, and others.

Do you remember hearing "Sea-Fever?"

I must go down to the seas again, to the lonely sea
  and the sky,
And all I ask is a tall ship and a star to steer her by.

This song of the sea was written by John Masefield who also penned a magnificent Christian poem, "The Everlasting Mercy," one you will want to share with your older children.

One can hardly forget Francis Thompson's "The Hound of Heaven," portraying so vividly man's flight from God:

I fled Him, down the nights and down the days;
I fled Him, down the arches of the years.

It's a great spiritual experience to share with your children. But long before they are old enough to understand the fascinating account of "The Hound of Heaven," they ought to meet Francis Thompson in "Ex Ore Infantium," one of my favorites:

> Little Jesus, wast Thou shy
> Once, and just so small as I?
> And what did it feel like to be
> Out of heaven, and just like me?

Ernest Thayer's "Casey at the Bat" or Robert Service's "The Cremation of Sam McGee" will capture the imagination of some who will have none of the mystical imagery of other verse. Explore, take time out to browse through good anthologies for children, and find some new joys for yourself as well.

The Psalms are rich in poetic melody.

> He who dwells in the shelter of the Most High,
> Who abides in the shadow of the Almighty,
> Will say to the Lord, "My refuge and my fortress;
> My God, in whom I trust."[3]

After you've read about the Red Sea incident, enjoy that wonderful song of Moses:

> I will sing to the Lord,
>   for he has triumphed gloriously;
> The horse and his rider
>   he has thrown into the sea.[4]

When reading of David's sin with Bathsheba, include Psalm 51:

> Have mercy on me, O God,
> According to thy steadfast love;
> According to thy abundant mercy
>   blot out my transgressions.[5]

Or the prayer of Moses, the man of God, in Psalm 90. Picture old Moses, leading the children of Israel, and listen:

---

[3]Psalm 91:1-2 RSV.
[4]Exodus 15:1 RSV.
[5]Psalm 51:1 RSV.

Lord, thou hast been our dwelling place
  in all generations.
Before the mountains were brought forth,
Or ever thou hadst formed the earth and the world,
From everlasting to everlasting thou art God.[6]

Jeremiah captures mankind's perpetual wandering:

For my people have committed two evils;
  they have forsaken me,
the fountain of living waters,
  and hewed out cisterns for themselves,
broken cisterns,
  that can hold no water.[7]

You will notice I have stuck closely to old favorites in this chapter on poetry, but that is not without purpose. They are favorites because people have loved them, and this is a good place to begin. Their lines sing, and their content is not obscure. As you move on into the world of poetry, you will find unfamiliar meter and blank verse, an irregular kind of prose called poetry. Don't be afraid to try it; it may fit your mood very well.

If you share poetry with your children, someday you will know the delight of their sharing favorites with you. I picked up our ninth grader one afternoon at school to take him to the barbershop for a haircut. He reached into his back pocket and drew out a sheet of notebook paper, folded many times, saying, "We studied this in school today, and I thought you'd like it." While he was getting his haircut, I sat in the car and read what he had bothered to copy for my enjoyment:

They are the slaves who fear to speak
For the fallen and the weak;
They are the slaves who will not choose
Hatred, scoffing and abuse,

---

[6]Psalm 90:1-2 RSV.
[7]Jeremiah 2:13 RSV.

> *Rather than in silence shrink*
> *From the truth they needs must think;*
> *They are the slaves who dare not be*
> *In the right with two or three.*[8]

Sharing makes for lovely companionship.

---

[8]James Russell Lowell, "They Are the Slaves."

6.

THE PLEASURE OF A
SHARED ADVENTURE

"If families don't read books together, how do they know each other's friends?"

That's exactly how we feel about it.

Reading aloud as a family has bound us together, as sharing an adventure always does. We do know the same people. We have gone through emotional crises together as we felt anger, sadness, fear, gladness, and tenderness in the world of the book we were reading. Something happens to us which is better experienced than described—a kind of enlarging of heart—when we encounter passages full of grand language and nobility of thought.

Much of our secret family idiom comes from the books we have read together. I say "secret" because a specialness surrounds it. You need to have shared the book to know what the phrase means, and when we use it, it's communication with the heart.

Sometimes it is silly doggerel like Horton's declaration of faithfulness in Dr. Seuss' *Horton Hatches an Egg:*

> *I meant what I said*
> *And I said what I meant,*
> *An elephant is faithful*
> *One hundred percent.*

Other times we speak of *Narnian air, the Ents, Barkis is willin', a useful pot for putting things in,* and hundreds of like phrases. When we went to visit a favorite spot and saw that much of what we remembered as beautiful had changed, our son said, "The orcs have been here," and we didn't need to say more.

We don't read a book to get a family vocabulary, you understand. It is just a cozy by-product worth mentioning only because of the intimacy of experience it expresses. That's the important part.

Not infrequently parents complain of inability to communicate with their children. "I cannot understand how he thinks!" I want to ask if they ever *really* thought together about ideas. Parents may treat children as *children* most of their lives—giving them "milk," working hard to provide opportunities for them—and then suddenly the children are on the verge of adulthood and they have never become acquainted with them as *people.* It is frightening to suddenly find people living in your household whom you don't know!

You can't one day decide to know your children and have it magically happen. You begin from the beginning by sharing "the honey" of life, as well as providing "the milk." Knowing someone means sharing ideas, growing together. It means not being embarrassed about feelings or being yourself. As a small boy, our son frequently commented, "I like him. He treats me like I'm a people." It's become a family joke, but being treated like "a people" means being taken seriously and being liked for who you really are. Interpersonal relationships within a family develop on this level.

At the age of seventy, Laurence Housman writes about the contribution reading made in his family in *The Unexpected Years:* "These family readings formed so satisfying a bond between older and younger that I can hardly think of family life without it; and I marvel when I hear of families in whose upbringing it has had no place."

In this day of committees and television, we don't marvel as Mr. Housman does, but we do recommend family reading with great enthusiasm for we have seen what it has done for our family and the immense pleasure and richness it has brought. Finishing the last book of Tolkien's trilogy was some of the most exciting reading we've ever done. A recent trip by car across the state was especially "delicious" because we were able to get extra chapters read as we drove along together. We share Mr. Housman's sentiments.

Family reading aloud demands good literature. Only the best can stand the test of having the words hit the airwaves and fall into the minds of such a variety of ages. You won't find a busy father reading insipid, sentimental stories aloud for very long—and the best family reading requires a father's voice. (That's a fact, however, not an excuse. Our father's work demanded that he travel, sometimes as much as 50 percent of the time. We kept a special book we only read when he was home, and another which we read when he was gone. But we always felt compelled to give him great, long summaries of what we were reading so he wouldn't feel left out!)

At the outset, with child number one, begin with the simple but good stories that were favorites in your own childhood or that you've recently discovered. While the

plot may not hold you as adults, something about it seems to come alive with freshness and gives what someone described as "a springtime urge to make them more beguiling than they ever sounded before."

Soon stories move into quite another class because children can understand far more than is sometimes guessed. When child number two comes along and is big enough to join the reading circle, if the favorites have been special literature they bear repeating, and no one minds. Each child deserves some catching up along the way, but do keep moving on up.

A family of four, ages five to twelve, read aloud together with the two older children in mind. The youngest, even if she doesn't always understand, feels the comfortable security of father's voice and of being included in the "inner circle." Sometimes she falls asleep in his arms, but she would rather be there with the family than in bed alone. Not infrequently the older children take special pleasure in re-reading past favorites with the younger ones, and that's a good kind of sharing, too.

"A book read aloud is a book better remembered, especially if the reading took place in childhood," writes William Henry Chamberlain in *Saturday Review*. "One of the first books my father read to me was that old, romantic war horse, *Ivanhoe*, by Sir Walter Scott. It has been decades since I last picked it up; but my memory, even for quite trivial incidents, is still quite keen. I can almost reconstruct from memory the language of the scene where a haughty Norman baron exclaims derogatorily, 'Your Highness may call me a Saxon!' to receive a prompt rebuff from stout old Cedric, the father of Ivanhoe, 'Who calls thee a Saxon will do thee an honor as great as it is undeserved.'"

Reading aloud doesn't allow anyone to set a speed record, but this is one of its advantages. How nice to amble together through the descriptive paragraphs, which might otherwise be raced past, and take a leisurely look around. One sees and feels more this way.

Characters seem more real when a story is read with some gift of expression. Maybe it is because a whole family is identifying with the characters and this strengthens the bonds one feels. Beautiful writing is seen more clearly to be what it is. We often interject, "That is magnificent!" or "What terrific insight!" And sometimes the reader gets such a large lump in his throat over the beauty or pathos of a situation that we all pause to swallow back our agony before going on. Who can read of Sidney Carton's vision of the future before he goes off to the guillotine in *A Tale of Two Cities* without a tear? Or of Aslan's marvelous reappearance after being killed in *The Lion, The Witch and The Wardrobe* without emotion?

I've already mentioned some of our favorite read-aloud books, but don't let these suggestions keep you from discovering others. We've read *Winnie the Pooh* more times than anyone would believe. Pooh books have a kind of wisdom and humor that gets better with the years. All of his friends are like people we know. As Poohphiles, we play Pooh Sticks on the bridge, we've gone on many an "expotition" to the North Pole, and we have wished to unbounce many a Tigger. It's annoying to see A. A. Milne's classic listed under a five-to-nine age bracket. Pooh is a collegiate favorite!

The Jungle Doctor series by Paul White of Australia has made good family reading. Dr. White is a superb story-teller in African fashion, and his stories excite both children and adults. As a modern-day Aesop, his *Monkey Tales* and *Jungle Doctor's Fables* speak a worldwide language, using the enchantment of animals to teach deeper lessons. Since he was formerly a missionary doctor, Paul White's stories are set in Tanzania and reflect the missionary and his message.

Patricia St. John's books have been read aloud at appropriate ages in our family. Our favorites were *Treasures of the Snow* (a Swiss setting) and *Star of Light*, which is a touching story of an unwanted girl in a Muslim home in Morocco and of her courageous brother.

Topping our best-reading list are the seven children's books by C. S. Lewis—the Narnia books, we call them. These seven gems have delighted us numerous times, each fresh reading providing new insights. What makes them so special? Excellent weaving of plot and characters into a most exciting, imaginative series of adventures, with the masterful skill of C. S. Lewis's style. But even more than this: the quality of the theme behind the stories!

The Narnia books are allegories and, as such, are rich in Christian thought. Profoundly Christian, the father in our house would say. Apart from the allegory, the books stand as superbly written adventure stories, and schoolteachers have held their classes spellbound with them without ever alluding to the allegory. Yet it is the allegory which has added the plus of pleasure for our family.

We began reading *The Lion, the Witch and the Wardrobe*, never mentioning what we as parents saw in the White Witch or in Aslan, the golden-maned Lion. Four children enter this magical land of Narnia which is under the rule of the White Witch—a land where it is always winter and never gets to Christmas. That is, until Aslan comes and brings spring and hope again. The children see Aslan captured by the witch, shorn of his majestic mane, tormented, and finally killed. We ached with the four children in their sadness, and then suddenly on the third day, Aslan is alive and comes bounding over the hill. At this point our seven-year-old couldn't get the words out fast enough in his excitement, "He's like the Lord Jesus. Aslan *is* the Lord Jesus!" What a wonderful moment. Aslan, the golden-maned Lion of the Tribe of Judah!

Each time we finished one book we were sure the next in

the series couldn't be as good. When we read *The Last Battle*, we felt we had been introduced to the most creative thinking about heaven we had ever done. Shortly after reading this, a neighbor boy, who had stayed overnight and thus been exposed to our family Bible reading at the breakfast table, commented, "I don't think I want to go to heaven. Who wants to sit around all day? I want to do something." What fun we had hearing our eight-year-old tell him that heaven wasn't going to be like that. Why, you could run with a unicorn and never get tired; you could even run up a waterfall, and the further in you got the better life tasted! If this sounds insane to you, then you'll have to read the book, and I hope you do.

The Wind in the Willows by Kenneth Grahame has been loved by children and adults for sixty years. Sometime around your child's eighth birthday, you ought to read it aloud together. The fellowship of Rat and Mole and Mr. Toad is too good to miss. Here again is an enduring quality of writing, rich in feeling and the author's commitment to the world he creates. When Ernest Shepard illustrated the story, he visited Kenneth Grahame in England, walking along the riverbank to make sketches of the setting for the story. "I love these little people," said Grahame. "Be kind to them. Make them real." And they do become real as you meet them in the story, and their sayings will surely become part of your family idioms. Who can forget the Christmas scene at Mole End, with the little mice, red mufflers wrapped around their throats, standing in a semi-circle outside, singing,

> *Villagers all, this frosty tide*
> *Let your doors swing open wide.*

The list of good read-aloud books is too long to continue carrying on in such detail, but I must mention some others.

C. S. Lewis was profoundly influenced by George Mac-Donald. *The Princess and the Goblin* and others by Mac-

Illustration by Ernest H. Shepard (copyright 1933 Charles Scribner's Sons, renewal copyright © 1961 Ernest H. Shepard) reproduced with the permission of Charles Scribner's Sons from *The Wind in the Willows*, page 92, by Kenneth Grahame.

Donald have the same kind of supernatural touch. As one young girl said, "I like these books the way I like the Narnia ones." Rich in wisdom, they are books your children should investigate.

Alice in Wonderland, Charlotte's Web, Mary Poppins, Dr. Dolittle, The Jungle Books—I hope you won't miss any of these.

When our children were about eleven years of age, or perhaps a little older, we went on to *David Copperfield, Oliver Twist,* and eventually *A Tale of Two Cities.* Charles Dickens's characters are magnificent; we know Wilkins Micawber, Lil' Emily, Peggotty, Uriah Heep, Oliver, and all the others. We didn't discuss these books as classics; we simply read them and enjoyed them.

At one point we read the unabridged edition of *Robinson Crusoe* together. My husband's freshman poetry teacher sent it to Mark as a gift, but it became a gift for my husband and me as well, because we had never read this as Defoe wrote it. We were outraged that a condensation had cheated us out of so much—even the seemingly dreary passages which describe the hopelessness of Crusoe's future on the island. Then one day Crusoe discovered a Bible in the bottom of an old trunk, and we saw the man we had known only as a shipwrecked victim become a believer in Jesus Christ. No child listening to this story could miss the convincing difference his conversion made in Crusoe's view of the island and life.

But do be wise in your choice of books. Don't force your children to appreciate any of these books. There are too many other good books to choose from which may meet their needs and yours more fully. Reading should be fun.

Reading J. R. R. Tolkien's *The Hobbit* and *The Lord of the Rings* has been an experience. Here is a masterful spinner of tales! We are awed by the power of language, the depth of characterization, the force of adventure. The test of good writing is the quality of the experience we receive in reading it. This is great writing! By all means, read Tolkien.

We finished the last book of the Tolkien trilogy, *The Return of the King*, on a wilderness canoe trip in the Canadian bush last summer. One morning when the wind was cold and strong, we huddled together in the largest tent to read. We were at such an exciting point in the book that it was easy to go on for several chapters. The tale was reaching its climax, the reader was having difficulty with the lump in his throat, and all of us had wet eyes over the sheer beauty of the scene of triumph after the destruction of the evil ring. If you haven't read the book, can you still feel with us the fulfillment of victory, of utter joy as the King comes into his own rightful place and all his warriors are honored?

> And all the host laughed and wept, and in the midst of their merriment and tears the clear voice of the minstrel rose like silver and gold, and all men were hushed. And he sang to them, now in the Elven-tongue, now in the speech of the West, until their hearts, wounded with sweet words, overflowed, and their joy was like swords, and they passed in thought out to regions where pain and delight flow together and tears are the very wine of blessedness.[1]

Later, when we prayed together by a moonlit shore, a seventeen-year-old thanked God not just for "beautiful things we can see, but for beautiful words which remind us of realities we cannot see."

While we have been tingling with excitement over these lengthy stories, I have thought repeatedly of Paul Hazard's word about "books that awaken in them (the readers) not maudlin sentimentality, but sensibility; that enable them to share in great human emotion; that give them respect for universal life—that of animals, of plants; that teach them

[1] J. R. R. Tolkien, *The Return of the King* (New York: Balantine, 1976), p. 286.

not to despise everything that is mysterious in creation and in men."[2]

I have mentioned two of the by-products of reading aloud: family closeness because of a shared experience and the bond of appreciation of good writing. The third factor has been alluded to: the opportunity of teaching what is true and good.

Cruelty, evil, and greed come into clear focus against kindness, truth, and honor in a well-written story. (I say well-written because nothing offends a child more than having to be told when something is mean and base or noble and good. This painful spelling out of what one is supposed to learn from a story evidences the author's inability to create valid characters in a real-life plot. And it insults children.)

The best teaching we have done in our family has been through reading the Bible and good books aloud together. It is really not such a profound concept. How would you best be enlightened to some truth—by being told that it was wrong to be nasty and thoughtless to others, or to meet and come to love some character in a story and then feel her hurts when someone is unkind and says cruel things?

We sometimes talk about the characters we meet in our stories and about the motivation behind their deeds. We discuss worthy ideas and try to hang important concepts into a larger framework of truth. The Christian parent who uses both the Book and books has a distinct advantage. The Bible spells out the precepts, the teaching of God's plan for man. It also tells us about real people—their faith, their sins, their courage, their disbelief—and we see the fruit of each in what follows in their lives. Good books fulfill our human need for adventure and wider experience, but they also provide support for the kind of character development of which the Scriptures speak.

---

[2]Hazard, Books, Children and Men.

When we meet a situation in a story where there is trouble and no faith, a child may say spontaneously, "Oh, if he only knew that God could help him!" Reading *The Adventures of Robin Hood* we discussed some pretty important issues when a tearful child asked, "Did Robin Hood go to heaven? He was such a good man." We didn't completely solve our mutual sorrow over Robin's death in the story, but some weightier matters were touched upon.

But deeper than this have been those elements of great strength of character and largeness of heart that I spoke of earlier. These are intangible things. One cannot drive a point home and say, "There he has learned that lesson." But by continual exposure to a variety of people and experiences, the real values of life are taught most profoundly.

Again, I recall a quote of Paul Hazard: "I like books that set in action truths worthy of lasting forever, and of inspiring one's whole inner life."[3]

What a pleasure to share that kind of a book with a child!

---

[3]Hazard, *Books, Children and Men.*

7.

HONEY FROM THE ROCK

MY GRANDFATHER was a Dutch immigrant with ten children. He and grandmother took seriously the instructions given by God in Deuteronomy 6, believing this to be a Christian parent's responsibility:

> These words which I command you this day shall be upon your heart; and you shall teach them diligently to your children, and shall talk of them when you sit in your house, and when you walk by the way and when you lie down, and when you rise. [1]

As the family gathered around the table for meals, one of my grandparents read from the Bible, usually three times a day. It was a kind of spiritual dessert. They had enjoyed

---

[1]Deuteronomy 6:6-7 RSV.

physical food from the hand of God; now they would enjoy spiritual food.

My father was one of these children. Later, when four small offspring sat around his table, he initiated the same practice. (As far as I know, his brothers and sisters have done similarly in their homes.) We never discussed whether or not we wanted to do this; it was just always done and never, to my knowledge, questioned. Reading material was chosen according to our ages. Often at the evening meal we read from a Bible storybook, but at least once a day we read short selections from the Bible. For some reason we read Proverbs more than any other single book; my parents must have believed that book contained an extraordinary amount of wisdom for everyday living.

To the children in our family this was a logical thing for a Christian family to do. No one left the table, unless for special reasons, until we read the Scriptures together. This was no legalistic ritual; it was family habit. Thinking back, I remember numerous instances when our friends called for us and we asked them to wait until we had finished dinner. Dessert may have been served, but none of us ever considered the meal finished until we had read together.

As I recounted this to a group of young couples recently, one father asked me, "Didn't you all grow up resenting your father and Christianity?" I felt an aching kind of amusement at his question.

"Quite the other way around," I answered. In all honesty, our parents and memories of family life are extra dear because of this. Four new families have come out of our parental home, involving fourteen children from four years to twenty-two, and each family follows the pattern we learned at home. Our expectations are that each of these fourteen will pursue a similar practice in their homes in years to come.

I laugh when I visit my brothers' homes and hear them stop in the middle of the reading to ask a child they suspect is not listening, "David, what was the last word?" That's what my father used to do. It will be fun to see if the grandsons use the same device.

Why is it that family Bible reading is such a rare thing in today's Christian homes, especially when it is the most alive, pertinent book in the world? Why did that young father expect that disciplined Scripture reading would produce resentment? Let me suggest several reasons.

1. Too many have a phony image of what this involves. Their minds conjure up pictures of a "family altar" with a large open Bible on the table against a background of flowers or a picture of Jesus. Around this scene, the family is piously kneeling for a minor church service each night. The people seem unreal, the language is that of Zion, and the experience looks as painful as possible.

But that image is a pretty shabby excuse for not making the Word of God central in our homes. Shouting about all of the abuses of the practice is hardly a creative exercise, and it doesn't fool God for one minute. We need less reaction and a good deal more action if our homes are going to stand the test of an increasingly secular world.

2. Parents are not really convinced of the importance of biblical instruction. *Not really*, I said. Because we do arrange for what we believe is important. Life is never so busy that we don't manage to see that our family has nourishing food, adequate clothing, and proper sleep. And, yes, we see that they get to Sunday school, church, youth organizations, and all the busy extras of life.

But parents who never read God's Word outside of an organized meeting of the church are not likely to sense the urgency of instructing children in the most important truth in the world. If we really believe that knowing God and His Son is the most vital experience in the world, how dare we leave the responsibility for instruction to someone else?

3. Parents lack the discipline that makes family life work. Parents need to live their lives with conviction, not hesitation. If you must make a fresh decision each day *whether* you will read the Scriptures and *when* you will read them, the Scriptures will probably not be read very often. Increasingly, Christian family life has little to distinguish it from secular family life.

Eating together and giving thanks for daily mercies should be a basic feature of our home life. In a discussion-growth group someone asked, "What was your favorite room in your family home?" I said without hesitation, "The breakfast room." That is where we ate our meals and were all together. We talked about the day, about our burning ideas, and shared our new jokes. Often one of our parents had to keep order by giving permission to speak because we all wanted to talk at once. No one left the table as soon as he had finished his food. Of course, I've already said that we read briefly at the close of the meal, but leaving would also mean that I didn't care what my brother was planning to do or what happened in my sister's day, an unthinkable lack of courtesy. Naturally we were nasty to each other on occasions, but this didn't change our family pattern.

I suppose there is nothing sacred about eating together in one sense, yet isn't it strange how important this was when believers met together in the New Testament? And just exactly where does one learn what it means "to practice hospitality" if it isn't around your own table, in your own home, with your own family? We prayed together, we ate together, we talked together. It was natural that we should read the Bible together. You may decide another time works better for you than mealtime; I only recommend this because I have seen it stand the test of three generations. It is a workable plan.

Breakfast time best suits our family for Bible reading.

(We usually are reading another book after dinner.) I dropped in at the close of dinner at my sister and brother-in-law's home the other day in time to join them for their Bible reading—five sons around the table, aged twelve to twenty-two. Dinner time works best for them.

Interestingly, we often reproduce in our homes the pattern we knew as children. Even those who complain bitterly about the deficiencies of their childhood family life often reproduce a pattern not noticeably different from the one against which they chafed. Others swing a full 180 degrees away from the past. Whether this is wisdom or rebellion depends on the quality of the motivation and the goals which are set.

Parents must decide what quality of family life they will have and then use the necessary discipline to accomplish this. Otherwise life will push the family in diverse directions, and they will be victims rather than disciples.

Ask a child if he wants to read the Bible after breakfast, and he may say no. Build it into the routine as naturally as drinking orange juice, and he will get proper nourishment. One of my favorite cartoons shows a child in a progressive school commenting to his teacher, "You mean I have to decide what I want to do!" When you are small and don't know what is valuable, that is an agonizing responsibility to place on a child.

I have mentioned the hindrances to family instruction at length because they are very real obstacles. It isn't enough to say, "Teach your children what the Bible says," thus adding to the burden of guilt parents already feel. Presumably, a fourth hindrance is that parents don't know how to begin. Isolating the problem is part of the solution.

Some time ago I listened to a panel of concerned Christian parents discuss the matter of "family devotions." Several on the panel mentioned their appreciation of the background given them by their parents. Yet not one of the families was successfully having any kind of regular biblical instruction in their own homes. Their reasons will sound familiar.

> They wiggle and squirm so much that we wonder what they get out of it anyway.
>
> We are just never all together when there is enough time.
>
> We have decided to wait until the children are older and want to participate more willingly.
>
> We try to do something special every now and then.

I listened and thought of my grandparents. With ten children I'm sure it wasn't always convenient to read the Bible, and there was plenty of wiggling. Grandfather probably didn't stop to psychoanalyze; he just did what he felt needed doing. I felt a rush of gratitude for a godly heritage. Because grandfather was faithful, my father was faithful, and we grew up in a home where we knew the importance and authority of God's revelation to men. We not only have a heritage; we are giving our children one. We decide what kind it will be.

But what if the father will not take the leadership? What if he is away from home much of the time? Many families flounder because of these societal patterns. The solution lies with the mother, who wisely takes over when she must, willingly passing leadership back to father at the first opportunity. Don't cancel something as important as Bible reading while waiting for more ideal circumstances. A child's life is too brief! My own father traveled away from home much of the time, and so does my husband. Not to carry on with something as vital to life as God's Word is like saying, "We won't eat any meals because dad isn't with us."

I must confess to a personal reaction against the words "family devotions" or "family altar." Maybe it is because these terms have a sentimental, somewhat unreal flavor. An "altar" is outmoded since the death of Christ. "Devotion" is what we have toward God all day long, not just during a family reading together. I want to build more content into this family time than these words allow me personally. But what we call it isn't as important as that we do it! So we simply refer to it as Bible reading.

But enough discussion about hang-ups which hinder us. Let's go on to a clear idea of our goal in Bible reading. Why is it so important? What are some meaningful ways to accomplish it?

The Goal

The goal of family Bible reading is to teach children to think biblically.

That's a large goal: to think biblically. It means a good bit more than quoting certain Scripture verses. It involves squaring up our thinking with what the Bible says about God, about man, about sin, about redemption, about human need, and about righteousness. Thinking biblically insists on an understanding of the fast sweep of what Scripture reveals to us. It is the gauge against which we measure our ideas and our lives.

How has God worked in human history? What is His goal? What is His essential nature, His character? What is the nature of man? What are his basic needs? How does the death of Jesus Christ fit into the picture? How do we know what is true? These are only some of the questions we answer in learning to think biblically.

The ability to quote salvation or assurance verses is inadequate unless the verses fit into a larger concept of the character of God and an understanding of His righteousness. Knowing favorite biblical heroes and specific stories becomes most meaningful when fit into a larger view of what their lives demonstrate about people or about God's character.

Parents, not uncommonly, invest time with small children, reading them favorite Bible stories and speaking of salvation. The failure comes in teaching children through

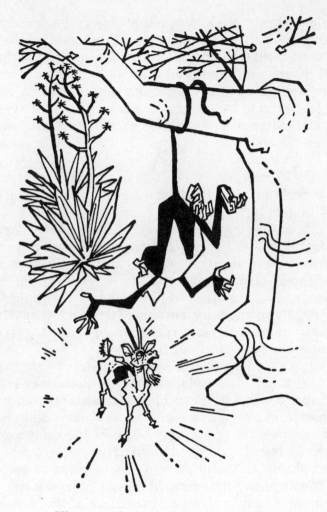

The goat who wanted to become a lion.

their teens how this information fits together to form a true philosophy for life. Our goal is a valid world-life view. This cannot be scolded into a person; we can only expose young minds to great truth and discuss it with them. The rest is God's responsibility as He works with us in our children's lives.

Our need for a word from God is never finished. He speaks to our situation, ministers to our problem areas. We receive fresh insights, daily reminders, new promises because the Word of God is indeed profitable "for teaching, for reproof, for correction, and for training in righteousness" (2 Tim. 3:16 RSV).

We demonstrate our confidence in the authority of the Word of God by the way we use it in our homes and by our personal obedience to it. No amount of emotional, cozy feeling will stand the rigorous test of university exposure. Our faith has intellectual content; we must know what we believe. Emotional warmth flows out of the application and obedience of these great truths.

Attaining the Goal

Check the bibliography for a number of books to help make instruction in godliness a delightful experience for children. Numerous beautiful, creative introductory books are available for younger ages. Begin early to teach your children about God and His Son by reading these stories together.

Stories which relate biblical teaching to real life give opportunity for in-depth discovery as children grow older. Often questions at the end of the chapter give children the fun of remembering and taking turns. *Little Visits With God* and *Devotions for the Children's Hour* are only two of many popular and excellent books. Explore the list and make generous use of the material available. You'll find yourself learning afresh as you teach your children.

Primarily, however, I'd like to share the idea that has

worked best toward attaining the goal in our family life. We have given this simple method thirteen years of trial and are pleased with its effectiveness in making the Bible meaningful.

When our son Mark was four years old, we began to read aloud from the Gospel of Mark. We chose this Gospel because of its name and because of its short narrative passages. Father had a plan. Everyone at the table (and this included our numerous guests) had to ask a question and answer one. He made a game of it. Sometimes the question was directed to the person on our left, other times to the person on our right. We'd have to listen carefully, and sometimes the question we had thought to ask was usurped by someone whose turn came first, and we would have to think of another.

At first our questions were simple. *Where did Jesus go? What did Jesus do? Who went with Jesus?* Mark picked up the idea rapidly. Then we began to interject another kind of question. *Why did Jesus say that? What does He mean?* And then later, *What can we learn from Jesus about the way we ought to act?*

In these questions are the three elements which open up any text: FACT—what does it say? INTERPRETATION—what does it mean? APPLICATION—what does it mean to me?

For a while Mark's questions centered on facts, but before long he began asking deeply penetrating ones. *If Jesus could raise Lazarus from the dead, why did He let His dear friend John the Baptist stay dead? Why did the Jews say Jesus had an evil spirit?* Increasingly we delved into the meat of what the text was saying.

Mark was delighted when father introduced a two-part question, and thereupon set out to explore the possibility of a three-part question. Together, as a family, we dug amazing truths out of the Word of God—and no one in our family would say this was either dull or painful.

This method requires that everyone think through what

the passage is saying. Ideas go through the thought processes and come out of the mouth. We experience a great thing: the joy of discovery. What is discovered for one's self is always more meaningful than that which is told by someone else.

It is exciting to see how the use of this method can become ingrained in a child's thought pattern and how this can enable him to take apart a piece of literature and comprehend what it is really saying. Children learn to listen, to isolate key ideas, to contrast and compare, and to come up with the heart of the text with the delight of a skindiver seeking a treasure on the ocean floor. Its benefits in our family have gone far beyond what we envisaged when we began this simple plan for Bible reading.

We have tried to handle the Bible honestly, letting it say what it says, not overly spiritualizing facts (which I believe turns children off because it lacks integrity and makes a sermon out of what isn't there!) The Bible is superb literature. It carries its own truth if we dig out the facts and apply them. We don't have to force its contents.

No need to attempt to protect truth, to explain away seeming inconsistencies either. Truth will turn out to be truth. We've tried to relate the Bible to everyday happenings, school studies, and new findings. When we've come upon words like fornication, circumcision, etc., we've talked openly about what these mean. If you have trouble explaining, look them up together in the dictionary. The Bible has adequate teaching about morality and sex for the twentieth century.

No other tongue in the world has the advantage of so many modern translations as we do! By all means, use contemporary English translations in your family Bible readings. So much of the message can be missed, avoided, or tuned-out when Elizabethan English is read. The other day a woman said to me, "I like to stick with the original Bible." I didn't bother to tell her she would have to learn

Greek and Hebrew to do that! The King James Version of the Bible was translated in 1611, and while its language flow is beautiful, particularly in the Psalms, young people deserve the privilege of hearing God's Word speak their own language in a twentieth century translation.

For those who are adventuresome, buy each member of your family an interlinear Greek New Testament to read together as your family matures. The English words appear above the Greek words, and one family we know has taught themselves the basics of Greek in this fashion.

All of us want the Bible to be a living Book for our children. One truth seems overwhelmingly obvious, however. No matter what technique we use, our own attitude is the key. We must be genuine. Our blatant inconsistencies linked with outward piety will battle the authority of the Word of God in our children's lives.

If we approach the Bible with a stained-glass window voice and emotional tremors that make the book seem "religious," in the most frightening sense of that word, chances are our children will escape at the first opportunity. Our prayers, too, must reflect that we are speaking with Someone who is real, not that we are making a speech.

The kind of family Bible reading I have been discussing is no rigid ritual that makes rules more important than people. On the contrary, it is because people—people God has given to us—are so very important that we are compelled to personal discipline in this matter. When we, as families, treat the Bible as "our necessary food," obviously respecting its authority by our own personal obedience, our children will find in this Book what they will never find in any other way: the way of eternal life—without which there can be no lasting enjoyment of God's gifts.

I have talked about many books in the preceding pages, books which will enrich a child's life. If you think my emphasis has been imbalanced—that I have put other books ahead of the Bible—you are mistaken. For at least eighteen years a child lives in our home. If he reads the Bible with us every day, what conclusion will he draw from our emphasis?

You will determine your child's attitude toward the Book and books by the paths you open up for him. And it will affect your children's children and the free, imaginative communication of the Good News of Jesus Christ in the years to come.

Illustration by N. C. Wyeth reprinted with the permission of Charles Scribner's Sons from *The Yearling* by Marjorie Kinnan Rawlings. Copyright 1939 by Charles Scribner's Sons.

8.

WHO INFLUENCES YOUR CHILDREN?

ABOUT 390 B.C. Socrates wrote about Athenian society:

> Could I climb the highest place in Athens, I would lift up
> my voice and proclaim, "Fellow citizens, why do you burn
> and scrape every stone to gather wealth, and take so little
> care of your children to whom you must one day relinquish
> all?"

Concern for the well-being of children and quality family life is not new! People must repeatedly be reminded
that societies do not disintegrate; families do. And when
family life fails, individuals experience deep loneliness
and disorientation. They look for someone to belong to
and grope for some idea worth believing in. I wonder if
there has ever been a time when individual young people
spent so much time discussing what kind of families they

come from or what the atmosphere of their home was like. They talk about it because they believe it explains them as persons.

Rarely does one hear of a couple seriously discussing together some kind of basic philosophy of family life — not a set of rules about how people must act or a contract of who will do what, but a concept of that bigger thing they want to build together. What is their concept of home, of family life? What should be its emotional tone, its intellectual atmosphere, its spiritual dimensions? What good thing can two people build together *for* and *with* their family that could never exist if each went his own way?

What is a home? Our favorite definition is *a home is a safe place*, a place where one is free from attack, a place where one experiences secure relationships and affirmation. It's a place where people share and understand each other. Its relationships are nurturing. The people in it do not need to be perfect; instead, they need to be honest, loving, supportive, recognizing a common humanity that makes all of us vulnerable.

A home that claims to be *Christian* has an extra plus: God at the center. He is the real head of the home, and all our inadequacies and fears are under His Lordship; our strengths and excitements are placed under His control. His love inspires ours; His forgiveness is the basis of our forgiveness of one another; His instructions are our guide. The claim to be a Christian family is not an easy boast one makes.

This affirmation of persons is no small thing. It is the heart of life. Each person needs to know and believe he is valuable and needs to have the self-esteem that comes with that deep inner assurance. Most profoundly we find our worth in the heart of God and in His love for us. But many people have difficulty believing God really loves them when they have been cheated from basic acceptance in their families. Tragically, some people spend most of their lives trying to prove their personal worth, trying to feel good about themselves. Their relationships suffer at every level because self's needs are so absorbing.

Virginia Satir, a family therapist, in her book *Peoplemaking* makes a flat statement based on years of observation of family life:

> In all troubled families I noticed that self-worth was low; communication was indirect, vague, and not really honest; rules were rigid, inhuman, non-negotiable, and everlasting; and the link to society was fearful, placating and blaming.
>
> In vital and nurturing families I consistently see a different pattern. Self-worth is high; communication is direct, clear, specific and honest; rules are flexible, human, appropriate and subject to change; and the linking to society is open and hopeful. [1]

This brings into focus our personal influence within our homes, and the spotlight settles on individual parents. Parents need basic self-esteem, for they set the pattern. Our influence flows out of our selves, our values, our priorities, and our basic understanding of the meaning of life. Parents need to make decisions to be as well as to do. What we are affects others significantly. Husbands and wives who affirm each other will be those who best affirm their children. Affirming, nurturing people influence others far beyond their intention simply because they provide rich soil in which individual personalities can grow.

Similarly, those parents who have carefully examined their values and their view of life are going to be those parents whose influence on their children is most consistent. Why? Because what they believe is important to them. Believing something is true means eliminating things which are not. Our priorities are determined by our values.

---

[1] Virginia Satir, *Peoplemaking*, (Palo Alto, CA: Science and Behavior Books, Inc. 1972), p. 4.

Jim didn't know.

"The answer is—a milk truck!" Paul said.

They all laughed. It was a good riddle.

From *The New Teacher* by Miriam Cohen, illustrated by
Lillian Hoban. Copyright © 1972 by Macmillan Publishing
Co., Inc. Reprinted with permission of the publisher.

Communication flows out of conviction. Far too many parents feel little responsibility beyond providing physical needs, seeing that order is kept and that their children are at the right places at the right time. They do not plan to be influencers of ideas, to furnish the mind with what is true. They expect the school and the church to do that for them.

On the other hand, some authoritarian parents believe that the word *influence* means propagandizing or dominating the spirit of another. You cannot bully people into appreciating what is true and good and beautiful. Out of sheer necessity to retain his own personhood, the independent spirit in a child will reject the parent who has "only my way to do it."

Influence does not mean overwhelming another person. Instead, it is being sure enough of what is true and good to have our actions (life style) and our words affect someone else. A word study here is interesting. The root meaning of *influence* has an astrological sense of *flowing into,* but in common usage it has come to mean *the exertion of action of which the operation is unseen, except in its effect.*

We influence by what we are and by what we do. In one sense, it could be said that we influence others simply by being. Yet we can all think of the colorless, inept teacher who did little to affect our lives, in contrast to the convinced, dedicated teacher who had goals and standards for herself or himself and, hence, for us.

Margaret Mead, in her book *Culture and Commitment,* writes about three kinds of societal patterns in American history. Essentially in the first, called post-figurative, the line of influence passes relatively unhindered from the grandfather to the father to the son. The grandfather expects the son's values to be the same as his own, even though he does not verbalize them. They work together, having limited contact with others outside the family, and

in the constancy of each other's company the influence is
effective. Perhaps this is best seen in pioneer America or in
television programs like "The Waltons" — and may even
still exist in some tightly knit ethnic groups.

The second pattern Mead calls co-figurative. With the
industrial revolution, the move to cities, and the consoli-
dated school, children came under new influence from
their peers. The voice of peers subdued the voice of parental influence. Stimulating one another, the young did what
their peers did and adopted habits and styles that caused
parents to wring their hands. Peer pressure was a force to
be reckoned with.

The third pattern, called pre-figurative, is a society with
thousands of voices crying out to be heard, with messages
to be received. Media pressure is added to peer pressure.
Communication experts say the average person sees about
800 to 1200 advertisements a day as he turns the pages in
magazines and newspapers, passes billboards, and hears
commercials — even though these may not be consciously
perceived. Add to this the onslaught of television programing with its varied propaganda regarding life styles,
the news, as well as those "good" programs we approve,
and you have a massive invasion of ideas into the head of a
young person.

Margaret Mead projects even greater changes and more
influences for the future. She concludes that no one has
ever lived in this kind of technological world before.
Therefore, she says, we cannot teach children what is
valuable because we don't know what is valuable for this
kind of world; we can only teach them the value of commitment. At this point Margaret Mead and I part company
(if, indeed, we ever were in company) because I believe we
do know what values are unchanging in a changing world.
And we can and must teach them to our children, or they
will have trouble extracting them from the babel of our
noisy environment.

My great concern is that parents are living in a pre-figurative world (to use Miss Mead's coinage) as though it were post-figurative. We must do more than live in the same house with our children. We need to spend time with them, talk to them, share our lives with them, and teach them. The words of God to the parents of Israel are significant: *When you sit in your house, and when you walk by the way and when you lie down and when you rise* (Deut. 6:7). Influencing our children is not a casual task. It won't get done unless we have a plan.

We can hardly dismiss the influence of television with a shrug. This media shapes our children's points of view and affects them emotionally, intellectually, and spiritually. Sociologists and psychologists conclude that anti-personal-relation values, anti-cooperation values, and anti-democratic values are communicated by television programing. In one hour the viewer may see more adventure, more violence, and more excitement than the average person experiences in a lifetime. People become spectators, detached from their own lives, almost refusing to take responsibility for living.

Parents and teachers report greater tension, anxiety, restlessness, and suspicion in children after prolonged television viewing. Children thrive on noise and confusion, and even strife. Short attention spans are almost inevitably the result of pre-school television programing that features an interruption every minute and a half. Children grow up seeing people break the law and beat the system on television. School authorities seem to believe this has lessened respect for all adult authority. Television often promotes hostility that children can't define, but they are then inclined to settle things with violence.

Personally, I have a strong negative reaction to Saturday morning television programs that congratulate children for having a day free from school in a way that implies escape from prison or some other miserable experience.

Geared to electronic sound and fury, children may feel that books and even conversations are rather dull unless they are helped to see otherwise.

Without question television consumes the largest part of the average American's free time. It is estimated that by age sixty-five most Americans have spent *nine years of twenty-four-hour days* in front of the television set. By the time a typical American boy or girl has reached the age of eighteen, he or she has totaled 12,000 to 15,000 hours of television watching. These are not hours stolen from school, but from relating to other people. It is not surprising that so many young people want to drop out of life. They don't know how to live it. Increasingly we observe that university students do not know how to relate well to other human beings.

Dr. Graham Blaine, chief psychiatrist in the student health services of Harvard University, has said that the most serious problem with television is not poor programming (although that is a subject worth discussion), but its destruction of the average family's exchange of views and information at the evening meal. People are anxious to get to a favorite program, he says, and so they hurry to finish eating. What happened during the day, little ideas or larger matters, are never discussed.

Further, we are now hearing statistics that indicate many families eat no more than three meals together a week. When does a family talk together?

When I hear university students say, "There's only so much time a person can spend with his parents," then I usually assume they aren't used to talking together as a family, sharing their lives, feeling together, or exchanging ideas. It is like saying there is only so much time one can spend with people. Parents are people, but some of them have never let their children know this. You can't wait to begin when they are grown up. You begin talking and sharing and listening when they are little.

We are inclined to make life heavy and see only what must be done, not what could be done. I suspect that as more and more mothers join the work force outside the home this burdened way of life will increase.

> The world is too much with us; late
>   and soon,
> Getting and spending, we lay waste our
>   powers:
> Little we see in Nature that is ours;
> We have given our hearts away, a sordid
>   boon![2]

We let the evening news take away our delight in the beauty of a sunset. The ugly becomes more real than the good. I think of G. K. Chesterton who once remarked that *God may be younger than we are.* He may say, "Let's have another sunrise." He delights in what He has made and is eternally creative. In the last part of the Book of Job, where God speaks, there are ten verses to the glory of the hippopotamus and thirty-four verses about the crocodile. God is not weighed down by the disorder man has brought to the world, wringing His hands as if life were out of control. Sometimes we take on burdens that belong to God.

Clyde Kilby, speaking about this, says the worse thing in the world is to believe that today is exactly like yesterday. Then we forget to notice and to share what is new and fresh and good about today.

What is worse, as we grow older, we have difficulty stretching our minds to connect what may be small, delightful, and everyday with what is big, eternal, and true. That's what children (and children's literature) can do for us. That's why talking and sharing are so important for grown-ups, not just for children. C. S. Lewis spoke of a child who on Easter morning was heard whisper-

[2]William Wordsworth, "The World Is Too Much With Us" (1806).

ing to himself, "Chocolate eggs and Jesus risen!" We need both the joy of chocolate eggs and Jesus risen in our lives.

Without this we become spectators of life, not feeling much, not expecting much, and always playing it safe. Truth and joy become the security of bank accounts instead of a sunrise or a bird's nest or a beautiful story. Increasingly, young people are trying to escape the sterile, safe world we create for them by backpacking, climbing, wilderness canoeing, and other stress experiences. Recently my husband was teaching a canoeing class at a camp for university students. When it began to rain gently, some in the class headed for shore. He called them back, reminding them that a little summer rain was good for everyone. Later one girl excitedly thanked him. "It was beautiful!" she said. "I was never allowed to be out in the rain on purpose when I was growing up. Instinctively I headed for shore until you called us back. The big raindrops hitting the flat, calm water and making bigger and bigger circles were just beautiful. And I love the feel of the rain on my face and in my hair." What was it that sparked such enthusiasm? The simple joy of experiencing a summer rain.

Underlying all of this discussion is my thesis that parents who read widely together with their children are going to be those who most influence their children, who have the largest world view, who have an uncommon delight in what is good and true and beautiful—and an uncommon commitment to it. Sharing and feeling and talking together will come naturally. Books shared with each other provide that kind of climate.

I can't prove it on a national scale, perhaps, but I'm a pretty convinced mother. When a son returns home from the university for summer vacation with two of his textbooks and says to his father, "I want to sell these but before I do I thought you and mother would enjoy reading the pages I've marked in them," then you know that sharing books is a two-way street.

When he phones and says, "Am I ever glad we read *That Hideous Strength* together last summer! I found myself in a situation this week in which I felt all the pressures to conform to the group and compromise my values to be part of the inner-ring. Then I remembered that story and the awful mistake it is to play the game that way"—then you have courage to boldly say to others that good books can influence behavior.

And when your husband finishes reading James Thurber's *The White Deer* aloud to you in bed one night, sighs, and suggests "we send it immediately for our married children to share," then you know that together you've set in motion a lifelong pattern that makes for rich living.

9.

MAKING DECISIONS ABOUT BOOKS

LANGUAGE IS an instrument; it is even more an environment, writes Norman Cousins. We create a climate with words. God spoke and created a world. On a different level, we also speak and create a world for our children.

Loving Conversations With the Young

Our words will be important to the children in our homes from the day they are born. Before a child is many weeks old he can distinguish one voice from another, and before many months he responds with his own jargon. Talking and singing or reciting nursery rhymes to him provides a warm atmosphere in which to grow.

Babies ought not to be bathed, dressed, or tucked into

115

bed in silence. Your own spontaneous conversation with them encourages them to respond with their own. They get used to the rhythm and joy of words. Nursery rhymes are a natural for this seeming one-sided dialogue in which you indulge yourself. The details of living bring to mind *Rub-a-dub-dub; One, two, buckle my shoe; Rockabye baby; Rain, rain, go away; Polly put the kettle on; Higgledy, piggledy, my black hen; Patti-cake.* I have a hunch Moses' mother sang such rhymes to him as she tucked him in his basket.

These "conversations" are important to children. I'm sure many three-year-olds keep asking *Why?* not so much out of intellectual curiosity as out of a desire to keep you talking. They feel good about conversation. You'll hear a child talk to his stuffed animals much the way you talk to him. If you talk down to him, he'll talk down to his animals. If you use baby talk, so will he. If your conversation helps him notice his environment, then you will hear him comment in this way in his monologues. You are building his vocabulary and enlarging his awareness by treating him as a person in your conversations.

That's how we begin, and although we're not consciously thinking about books when we hold these loving conversations with the young, we are getting a child ready to read. Words are important. Picture books that tell a story will follow naturally, and sooner than you realize a child will begin to "read" the pictures and make up his own story. *Do You Want To Be My Friend?* by Eric Carle is a favorite book without words. It begins with a small gray mouse asking the question and then leading the reader through the pages. *Four Frogs in a Box* by Mercer Mayer can be "read" by children as young as two.

Plan a regular read-aloud time with your child. Few activities are as rewarding as this in creating a warm relationship. There is a good feeling in sharing a story at any age. The reading list at the back of this book begins with books to be read to the very young. Children who are read to from the very first come to expect that a book brings pleasure, that letters make words, that words put together in the right way say something that is fun.

Building Your Child's Library

At two years old your child may become possessive. He needs books that belong to him. Even the size and shape will be important to him. He will have favorites that he looks at hundreds of times and greets as old friends. As he grows older, he will want more. How do you decide which books to buy? A person does need to own some books—choice volumes that become part of one's life. No borrowed book or library book will have quite the influence as one that is owned, especially at a young age.

Give books as gifts, and be prepared to pay the price for them. The worst kind of books to buy are often those found on grocery store racks and will encourage impulse buying. They aren't quality stories for the most part (if you read them aloud, you'll realize this) and make no lasting contribution to a library.

On the other hand, our sixteen-year-old nephew recently wrote us a thank-you letter for a gift, our latest contribution to his library (the C. S. Lewis trilogy), and in his own inimitable way expressed appreciation for every addition we'd made to his library from the very first. He put an asterisk next to that sentence and footnoted at the bottom of the page: *Age three: A Hole Is to Dig, and I still remember you reading it to me.* A good book makes a lasting impression! Can you imagine him commenting on a gift of clothing or a toy thirteen years later?

Of course you will begin with a good nursery rhyme book by a good illustrator. Don't get a flimsy, common one. Buy one that is really beautiful, one the child will want to pass on to his or her children!

A child needs some picture books that say "good-night"

Lyle was always one for sharing.

or talk about the child's world in a way that makes him feel safe and loved. Be sure to include at least one good poetry book (and buy a new one for each major shift in comprehension) and read it aloud. Next you'll add a few storybooks like *Little Toot* by Hardie Gramathy or the *Mr. Small* books by Lois Lenski or *Mike Mulligan and His Steam Shovel* by Virginia Burton or *Make Way for Ducklings* by Robert McCloskey. Take the bibliography in this book with you when you go to the store and look the books over carefully. You won't be able to buy them all, and some will obviously appeal to you more than others. You will know what is just right for the child you have in mind. Trust your judgment.

Children love animal books: first picture books, then storybooks about animals. The *Frances* series, *Lyle, Lyle Crocodile, George and Martha, Where's Wallace?* and many others are in this category.

The paperback bonanza puts many of these good books within reach of our pocketbooks. Children's books are often unusually expensive, largely because of the colored illustrations. These new paperbacks mean that every child can own more. The good paperbacks are printed from the same plates as the original hardcover editions, sometimes with fewer color plates. Children like paperbacks and often choose them over hardcover editions because they are soft and more flexible. As one child remarked, "This book seems more friendly."

However, the binding will not last as long on a paperback, and you will want certain special books in hardcover. One of these is the classic *The Wind in the Willows.* I'm especially fond of Scribner's anniversary edition with illustrations by Ernest Shepherd. We read this aloud in our family at about age eight. Later at age eighteen it was pulled off the shelf again with the comment, "I'd forgotten how really good this book is!" Worth reading at age eight and worth reading at eighteen.

How can you tell which ones to buy in hardcover? The answer may vary with your family tastes. Part of the answer is in the lasting quality of the story. I think *Winnie-the-Pooh* is worth hardcover; C. S. Lewis's *Narnia Chronicles*. *Alice in Wonderland*, and others like this that have stood the test of time. But that also reflects our family tastes. Yours may be different. If a book will only be read once or twice and then pass into oblivion, then a paper edition will do.

Giving books as gifts is an important way to build a library, but the child needs also to develop a sense of ownership and pride in his own library. As he grows older, let him help you choose books and discuss with him why you don't buy some books on impulse, even if all you say is, "Let's buy a really *good* book." You are helping him decide on quality. Treating books carefully and returning them to the special place where books are kept is an important part of owning his own library.

Many families set aside money to buy at least one book a month. It should be a family project. Sometimes your children may decide to buy a book they have already read from the library because the experience in reading it was so fine that they want to own it. That is like choosing an old friend to be with you forever.

If you are isolated from a bookstore that carries a large selection of children's books, use the library to decide what you want and then order it through any book department in a major store. The children's librarian will also be able to furnish you with sources. The school child is soon introduced to a variety of book clubs, most of these paperback clubs. Generally the prices are good. *Weekly Reader* and *Scholastic Book Clubs* have good selections that include fun books like *Pippi Longstockings* or *Homer Price*. Books that span several age levels or the classics are less likely to be offered. However, whatever the book club, don't take consistent quality for granted. Look them over.

As independence and reading interest grow, take your child with you to the book fairs where secondhand books are sold. Both of you must be able to recognize authors and the books you would really want to own to make this profitable. I have known children to find beautifully bound editions of *Moby Dick, Tom Sawyer,* or *Treasure Island* on such excursions.

One book is a must: a dictionary—a good dictionary with large enough print to invite reading. If you can afford it, *The Random House Dictionary* is first-rate and goes beyond an ordinary dictionary to include some details found in an encyclopedia. It's a big book and must be kept accessible.

Make "looking it up" a family habit. We keep a dictionary near our dinner table so that in the course of discussion it is easy to verify meanings and learn new things. It doesn't have to be a big dictionary. *Webster's Collegiate Dictionary* will do as well. Every home should have one handy. Dictionaries make wonderful graduation gifts for a personal library later on.

We think a good atlas needs to be part of a standard family library. We have the *National Geographic World Atlas* that allows us a careful look at the far places of the world. The evening news becomes more meaningful, as well as places mentioned in other books we read.

Using the Library

A trip to the library should be at least a bimonthly affair. You will want your child to enjoy far more books than you can buy. Almost all libraries have extensive children's sections, and a library card becomes an important possession. Begin visiting the library together at an early age, and allow plenty of time to look and choose.

Notice authors and illustrators, and call your child's attention to them. That's the first step in beginning to find your way in a library. A child who feels at home in a library at a young age will be one who uses the library all his life.

Don't be afraid to check out as many books as the library allows. You will make some good selections, while some will be less appealing when you get them home. That's how you learn what to look for and help your child learn as well. A library can be intimidating and can make a person feel uncertain about actually making a selection. But you haven't lost anything if your choice turns out to be disappointing. You aren't committed to read it, and next time you will be wiser.

How to Use a Book List

Some say that mediocre reading material doesn't hurt a child, but childhood is brief, and without some guidance a child may miss what is quality reading and never discover the pleasure of a well-written book. It seems wisest to pack all the goodness we can into the formative years.

A book list is as good as the understanding of the person who compiled it. Book lists for preschoolers through grades three are generally in agreement. Lists for older readers may sometimes reflect the compiler's view of what it means to be contemporary or relevant (see Fantasy and Realism).

I've tried to avoid all questionable reading in this book list and to include primarily those books that would both delight and benefit children. Not every good book is included. You may ask, "Why did she leave this one out?" I may have missed it, or it was simply left out in the process of selection. Of the writing of books there is no end! I couldn't include everything, but I have tried to list those books that will still be considered superior reading ten years from now.

Listing books according to age is risky because maturity and reading levels vary so much. (Do be careful not to let your child miss the good books which fit his particular age in your urgency to see how advanced he is in reading!) I have divided the reading lists into categories:

Good Reading—General
Poetry
Christmas Stories
Books to Help You Grow as a Christian

Within each category there are three major age divisions:

I Preschoolers through Grade 3
II Middlers (Grades 4–6)
III Teens and Mature Readers

Books are generally listed from easier to more advanced reading within each section. The annotations on the books are of necessity very brief. Each deserves far more enthusiastic comment than I've included, but it is hard to do justice to plot and characters in two sentences.

The best way to use this bibliography is to take the book with you to the library or the bookstore and browse around. For instance, if you are interested in purchasing a Mother Goose book, compare the various editions and choose one that pleases you most.

Become familiar with authors and illustrators. Sometimes you will notice that an author/illustrator you like is the illustrator of a book by another author. That may be your clue to investigate a new author. Children's books are a wonderful education, and you will soon begin to feel at home in this realm and find yourself talking books at home and with other parents.

Often the parent most enthusiastic about books is the father. Once he is captured by the fun of children's literature, he sees that the budget has money for books and takes his turn going to the library. If the father in your home isn't on this wavelength yet, don't just assume he won't ever be interested. Whet his appetite in all the ways you can, because books are a family affair.

Various medals and awards are given each year by several societies for the best books published. Two of the most familiar are *The Caldecott Medal* and *The Newbery Award*. The *Caldecott* has been awarded annually since 1938 to the artist of the most distinguished picture book for children during the preceding year. The award is named for Ralph Caldecott, the famous illustrator of books for children. The *Newbery* has been awarded annually since 1921 to the author of the most distinguished contribution to American literature for children during the preceding year.

Don't let a medal or an award dictate your reading, however. Some are clearly better than others, and always there is the dimension of personal interest.

I could wish you nothing better than that you will be a joyful dispenser of "honey" to those you love. Happy reading!

Bibliography

Many of the following titles are available in both hardcover and paperback, and many are available in several editions by various publishers. If a particular edition or illustrator is recommended, it has been indicated. You can find the publisher or publishers of these books by checking in *Books in Print* (R. R. Bowker Co., publisher) at your library or local bookstore. Books are listed according to complexity, rather than alphabetically.

Good Reading I—Preschoolers Through Grade 3

Mother Goose, ill. by Tasha Tudor.
Seventy-seven favorite nursery rhymes with colored illustrations.

Book of Nursery and Mother Goose Rhymes, ill. by Marguerite de Angeli.
The illustrations make this book special. Contains 376 rhymes.

Mother Goose, ill. by Kate Greenaway.

Mother Goose, ill. by Gyo Fujikawa.

The Tall Book of Mother Goose, ill. by Feodor Rojankovsky.

The Great Big Animal Book, ill. by Feodor Rojankovsky.

Garth Williams, *Baby Animals*, ill. by author.
Animals, loving pictured, made for small hands.

Margaret Wise Brown, *Goodnight Moon*.
A soothing sleepy-time story.

Charlotte Zolotow, *The Sleepy Book*, ill. by Vladimir Bobri.
Just right for reading at bedtime to the very young.

Margaret Bloy Graham, *I Love You, Mouse*, ill. by de Paola.
A loving good-night book for the very young.

Sylvia Plath, *The Bed Book*.
What is your bed like? Imaginative and homey.

Ring-o ring o'roses.

Ruth Krauss, *The Bundle Book*.
A loving story of a little one's bedtime game with his mother.

Polly B. Berends, *Who's That in the Mirror?*
A child learns to identify himself in the mirror.

Alvin Tresselt, *White Snow, Bright Snow*.
Puts into words and pictures the marvel of a snowfall. Caldecott Medal.
———, *The Beaver Pond*.
———, *Hide and Seek Fog*, ill. by Roger Duvoisin.
———, *The Mitten*, ill. by Yaroslava.
An old Ukranian folk tale.

Marjorie Flack, *Angus and the Cat*.
Angus is a Scotch terrier who has some merry adventures with a cat.
———, *The Story About Ping*.
A little Chinese duck and his adventures on the Yangtze River.
———, *Ask Mister Bear*.
———, *Walter, the Lazy Mouse*.

Beatrix Potter, *The Tale of Peter Rabbit*, ill. by author.
This and 22 other volumes are miniature books which are all-time favorites. Should be among a child's first books.

Wanda Gag, *Millions of Cats*.
A wonderful picture book about an old man looking for a cat.

Ezra Jack Keats, *The Snowy Day*.
A story of Peter's great fun in a snowy world. Caldecott Medal.
———, *Peter's Chair*.
A gentle story about jealousy over a new family addition.
———, *Goggles*.
———, *Hi, Cat!*

Charlotte Zolotow, *Do You Know What I'll Do?*, ill. by Garth Williams.
A child's wishes for her new baby brother.
———, *Big Sister and Little Sister*.

Brian Wildsmith, *Brian Wildsmith's Animals.*
An experience in color and charm.
_____, *Brian Wildsmith's Circus.*
_____, *The Little Wood Duck.*
_____, *The Lazy Bear.*

Mercer Mayer, *Four Frogs in a Box,* ill. by author.
No words, just engaging pictures that tell a story. Four books in a slipcase. A charmer.
_____, *One Monster After Another.*

Old Woman and Her Pig, ill. by Paul Galdone.
Old Mother Hubbard and Her Dog, ill. by Paul Galdone.
The Monkey and the Crocodile, ill. by Paul Galdone.
The Little Red Hen, ill. by Paul Galdone.
The above four are old nursery tales beautifully illustrated in an appealing format.

Eric Carle, *Do You Want to Be My Friend?*
Wordless book where the end of an animal's tail appears on each page; the child must guess what animal before the page is turned.
_____, *Very Hungry Caterpillar.*
The caterpillar is so hungry he eats right through the pictures in the book.
_____, *Have You Seen My Cat?*

Charlotte Zolotow, *William's Doll,* ill. by William Pene du Bois.
William wants a doll so he can practice being a father.
_____, *It's Not Fair.*
_____, *The Storm Book.*
_____, *Hold My Hand.*
_____, *May I Visit?*
_____, *The Quarreling Book.*
And many others.

Richard Scarry, *The Early Bird.*
_____, *Richard Scarry's Please and Thank You Book.*
_____, *Richard Scarry's Best Word Book Ever.*
_____, *Richard Scarry's Storybook Dictionary.*
_____, *Richard Scarry's What Do People Do All Day?*
All Scarry's books are full of detailed pictures children love.

Hardie Gramatky, *Little Toot.*
    An old favorite. A mischievous little tugboat becomes a hero.
———, *Hercules.*
    A horse-drawn fire engine comes out of retirement.

Lois Lenski, *The Mr. Small Books.*
    Papa Small is proud of his three little Smalls. This series
    includes *Policeman Small, The Little Train,* and others. Lois
    Lenski is a name to remember.

Virginia Burton, *Mike Mulligan and His Steam Shovel.*
    A race against time as Mike and his steam shovel dig a cellar.
———, *The Little House.*
    Story of a house in the country and the changes the years
    bring as the city moves closer. Caldecott Medal.

Robert McCloskey, *Make Way for Ducklings.*
———, *Time of Wonder.*
———, *One Morning in Maine.*
———, *Blueberries for Sal.*
———, *Lentil.*
    McCloskey is a favorite author and illustrator you and your
    children should meet. His books have a special touch that
    delights children. Look for his books for older readers as well.

Alice Goudey, *The Day We Saw the Sun Come Up.*
    A lovely book which captures the wonder of sunrise. Look for
    Goudey's books on nature for older children as well.

Janice Udry, *A Tree Is Nice.*
    Happy feelings about the delights of a tree. Caldecott Medal.
———, *What Mary Jo Shared.*

Ruth Krauss, *A Hole Is To Dig: A First Book of First Definitions,*
    ill. by Maurice Sendak.
    A collection of active definitions for preschoolers, such as
    "Hands are to hold."
———, *Open House for Butterflies.*

Don Freeman, *The Chalk Box Story.*
    Story of crayons who escape to create a lovely picture.
———, *Corduroy.*
———, *Dandelion.*
———, *Norman the Doorman.*

———, *Mop Top.*
———, *The Seal and the Slick.*
An ecology book.

Clarence W. Anderson, *Billy and Blaze.*
Series adventures of a boy and his pony.

Russell Hoban, *Frances Books*, ill. by Garth Williams and Lillian Hoban.
A series about a lovable badger, full of tricks, who learns many good lessons.
———, *Harvey's Hideout.*
And many others.

Margaret B. Graham, *Benjy's Dog House.*
Benjy has his own ideas about where to sleep.

Beatrice S. De Regniers, *May I Bring a Friend?*
The king and queen invite a small boy to tea, and each time he brings one of his friends—a seal, a hippopotamus, and lions. Caldecott Medal.
——— and Irene Haas, *A Little House of Your Own.*
Suggests places a child can have a secret house.
——— and Isabel Gordon, *The Shadow Book.*
Shows how to creatively use shadows.

George Mendoza, *Herman's Hat*, ill. by Frank Bozzo.
When Herman has his hat on, no one can ever tell what he is thinking.

Betsy C. Byars, *Go and Hush the Baby.*
A clever young boy helps his mother by quieting the baby.

Bernard Waber, *Ira Sleeps Over.*
A little boy is invited to a friend's home to sleep and wonders if he should take his teddy bear.

Lore Segal, *All the Way Home*, ill. by James Marshall.
Picture story of a city mother bringing two howling children home from the park and all the creatures who join the procession.

Eleanor Clymer, *Not Too Small After All*.
Joey, too small to be in the big boy's game, wins a place in their esteem.

Hilary Knight, *Where's Wallace?*
A fun book about an orangutan who escapes from a zoo.

Countee Cullen, *The Lost Zoo*.
A poet and his cat tell why certain strange animals are never seen in zoos. New edition by Follett, imaginative illustrations.

Tasha Tudor, *Corgiville Fair*, ill. by author.
Sights and fun of a small-town fair and a goat race!

William Pène du Bois, *Bear Circus*, ill. by author.
Koala bears put on a circus to say thanks to a kangaroo. Excellent illustrations.

Edward Ormondroyd, *Theodore*, ill. by John M. Larrecq.
A toy bear accidentally gets washed and is not recognized until he gets dirty again.
_____, *Broderick*.
A story of a young mouse who rides the surf.

Leo Lionni, *Frederick*.
Frederick doesn't gather food for winter like the other mice, but when winter comes and the food is almost gone, he shares what he has.
_____, *Swimmy*.
_____, *Alexander and the Wind-Up Mouse*.
A favorite!
_____, *Inch by Inch*.
_____, *Fish Is Fish*.
_____, *The Biggest House in the World*.

May Garelick, *Where Does the Butterfly Go When It Rains?*, ill. by Leonard Weisgard.
Beautifully illustrated and a good story line.

Judy Delton, *Two Good Friends*.
_____, *Two Is Company*.

James Marshall, *George and Martha.*
George and Martha are two friendly hippos who have a true friendship.
_____, *George and Martha Encore.*
_____, *George and Martha Rise and Shine.*

Charles and Ann Morse, *Whobody There?*
All children know "whobodies" who teach them things they need to know.

Robert Kraus, *Owliver.*
Oversize book about an owl whose father wants him to be a professional man instead of an artist.
_____, *Leo the Late Bloomer.*
_____, *Milton the Early Riser.*
_____, *Whose Mouse Are You?*

Marie H. Ets, *Play With Me.*
A little girl learns how to win friends. A book of real beauty.
_____, *Gilberto and the Wind.*
_____, *Just Me.*

Nancy Jewell, *The Snuggle Bunny.*
Warm story of a snuggle bunny who finds a lonely old man to snuggle against.
_____, *The Family Under the Moon.*

William Steig, *Sylvester and the Magic Pebble.*
Sylvester finds being together with people he loves more important than material possessions.
_____, *Roland the Minstrel Pig.*
_____, *Amos and Boris.*
_____, *Abel's Island.*
_____, *The Amazing Bone.*

Taro Yashima, *Umbrella.*
A Japanese girl longs for a rainy day so she can use her umbrella.
_____, *Crow Boy.*
A story that teaches acceptance of others who are different.

Elizabeth Hill, *Evan's Corner,* ill. by Nancy Grossman.
The story of a child's search for a place of his own and his

mother's ingenuity in showing him that their apartment has
eight corners—one for him and each member of the family.

Uri Shulevitz, *Rain Rain Rivers*, ill. by author.
Snug indoors, a little girl watches the rain and thinks of the
fun she will have tomorrow. Lovely illustrations express the
mood of a rainy day.
_____, *One Monday Morning*.
_____, *Oh What a Noise*.

Nancy Willare, *Simple Pictures Are Best*, ill. by De Paola.
A funny story of a family trying to get just the right photo-
graph.

Hans A. Rey, *Curious George*.
A small monkey finds himself repeatedly in difficulty. Look
for other books in the series.

Gene Zion, *Harry the Dirty Dog*, ill. by Margaret Bloy Graham.
Harry hates to have a bath, so he gets so dirty no one recog-
nizes him. Very funny adventures continued in several other
books.

Verna Aardema, *Why Mosquitoes Buzz in People's Ears*, ill. by
Leo and Diane Dillon.
Unusual illustrations. Caldecott Medal (1976).

Rebecca Caudill, *A Pocketful of Cricket*.
A pet cricket goes to school in a small boy's pocket.

Dr. Seuss, *Horton Hatches an Egg*.
_____, *And To Think That I Saw It on Mulberry Street*.
And many others. Dr. Seuss's books are full of imaginative
creatures and situations.

Claire H. Bishop, *Five Chinese Brothers*.
Five identical brothers who save each other's lives by one
distinguishing trait each possesses.

Maurice Sendak, *Nutshell Library*.
Four tiny books in a slipcase, full of fun and learning:
*Alligators All Around; Chicken Soup with Rice; One Was
Johnny; Pierre*.
_____, *Where the Wild Things Are*.

Sendak is an author and illustrator to remember when looking for imaginative books. Caldecott Medal.
———, *Seven Little Monsters*.
———, *Hector Protector*.
———, *Higglety, Pigglety Pop: Or, There Must Be More to Life*.

Barbara Cooney, *Chanticleer and the Fox*.
Geoffrey Chaucer's "Nun's Priest Tale" adapted by the illustrator. Caldecott Medal.

Munro Leaf, *The Story of Ferdinand*, ill. by Robert Lawson.
A story of a bull who favored smelling flowers to facing the toreador
———, *Wee Gillis*.
A delightful story of a Scottish boy.

Sesyle Joslin, *What Do You Say, Dear?*, ill. by Maurice Sendak.
———, *What Do You Do, Dear?*
Humorous handbooks on manners for very young ladies and gentlemen.

Alice Dalgliesh, *The Bears on Hemlock Mountain*.
Thrilling story of a boy sent over the mountains to borrow a kettle.

Lynd Ward, *The Biggest Bear*.
Johnny wanted a bearskin on his barn so he went looking for the biggest bear. Caldecott Medal.

Byrd B. Schweitzer, *Amigo*, ill. by Garth Williams.
Francisco longs for a pet and finds a wild prairie dog who wishes to tame a boy. Delightful story.

Rumer Godden, *Mouse House*.
———, *The Old Woman Who Lived in a Vinegar Bottle*.

Carmen B. De Gasztold, tr. by Rumer Godden, *Prayers from the Ark*.

Bernard Waber, *Lyle Crocodile*.
Adventures of a pet crocodile who thinks he is a person. Look for others in series, including *Loveable Lyle*.

Jemima shares her troubles with the gentleman fox.

Wesley Dennis, *Flip*.
A lovable colt has a dream of flying, and after that he jumps the streams more easily.

Miriam Cohen, *Will I Have a Friend?*, ill. by Lillian Hoban.
Jim is anxious about entering school. Well-done.
———, *Best Friends*.
———, *The New Teacher*.

Brinton Turkle, *Thy Friend, Obadiah*, ill. by author.
A little Quaker boy on Nantucket becomes a friend of the sea gull he helps.

Adelaide Hall, *The Runaway Giant*, ill. by Mamoru Funai.
A story about winter, a mysterious giant, and the excitement of discovering who it is.

Margaret Wise Brown, *The Steamrollers: A Fantasy*, ill. by Evaline Ness.
Daisy's parents give her a steamroller for Christmas (an obvious selection!), and she goes out and uses it! Nervy and funny.
———, *Fox Eyes*, ill. by Garth Williams.

Peggy Parish, *Amelia Bedelia*.
Amelia is a new maid, eager to please, with silly results. Look for others in the series.
———, *Granny and the Indians*.
Another series. Delightful.

Syd Hoff, *Albert the Albatross*, ill. by author.
A strange bird finds the ocean by traveling on a lady's hat. Easy reading for beginners.
———, *Julius*.
———, *The Horse in Harry's Room*.
———, *Sammy the Seal*.
———, *Danny and the Dinosaur*.
———, *Syd Hoff's Joke Book*.
———, *Walpole*.

Else H. Minarik, *A Kiss for Little Bear*, ill. by Maurice Sendak.
———, *Little Bear*.
———, *Little Bear's Friend*.

Humorous adventures of a mother bear and a little bear. Can be read by many first graders.

Norman Bridwell, *Clifford the Big Red Dog*, ill. by author.
Another series of books full of fun. Good for young readers.

Arnold Lobel, *Frog and Toad Are Friends*.
_____, *Frog and Toad Together*.
_____, *Frog and Toad All Year*.
Tender affection between Frog and Toad pervades these simple stories with amusing art by the author.
_____, *Mouse Soup*.
_____, *How the Rooster Saved the Day*.

Philip D. Eastman, *Are You My Mother?*
Story about a baby bird in search of its mother. First reader.
_____, *Flap Your Wings*.
Story of a little boy who puts an alligator egg in a bird's nest.
_____, *Go, Dog, Go!*
_____, *Sam and the Firefly*.

Bernard Waber, *You Look Ridiculous Said the Rhinoceros to the Hippopotamus*.
_____, *An Anteater Named Arthur*.

Edna Becker, *Nine Hundred Buckets of Paint*.
An old woman, her two cats, her donkey, and her cow set out to find a suitable home.

Roger Duvoisin, *Petunia*, ill. by author.
Funny story of a goose that finds a book and begins putting on airs. Also look for *Petunia Takes a Trip*, *Petunia's Christmas*, and others.

Jean M. Craig, *The New Boy on the Sidewalk*.
Joey and his new neighbor come to understand each other in this realistic urban setting.
_____, *The Dragon in the Clock Box*.

Tomi Ungerer, *Crictor*, ill. by author.
Hilarious picture story of a boa constrictor which is the pet of an elderly French schoolmistress.
_____, *The Beast of Monsieur Racine*.
_____, *No Kiss for Mother*.

Evaline Ness, *Exactly Alike*, ill. by author.
Having four freckle-faced brothers exactly alike is almost too much for Elizabeth.

John Burningham, *Seasons*.
Beautiful tracing of activities through the seasons.
———, *Mr. Gumpy's Outing*.
Mr. Gumpy takes children and farm animals for a boat ride and tells them "not to flap about," but they forget.

Ludwig Bemelmans, *Madeline*.
———, *Madeline's Rescue*.
Inimitable Madeline and her adventures make for hilarious reading. Three other Madeline books are in the series. Caldecott Medal.

Evaline Ness, *Sam, Bangs and Moonshine*.
Story of how a little girl learns to distinguish truth from "moonshine." Caldecott Medal.

Leo Politi, *Song of the Swallows*.
Juan rings the mission's bells to welcome the swallows back. Politi's illustrations have a warmth and gentleness appealing to children. Caldecott Medal.
———, *Moy Moy*.

Marcia Brown, *Stone Soup*.
An old tale about the lesson three soldiers taught the villagers.
———, *Dick Whittington and His Cat*.
———, *The Three Billy Goats Gruff*.

Carl Memling, *A Gift-Bear for the King*.
It's the king's birthday, and an old man and woman send him a little bear cub.

David L. Harrison, *Book of Giant Stories*, ill. by Philippe Fix.
Good stories, marvelous art—a treasure of a book to own.

Rebecca Caudill, *The Best-Loved Doll*.
Betsy's doll wins a prize, even though she is very worn, for being best-loved.
———, *Did You Carry the Flag Today, Charley?*

Charles Kingsley, *The Water-Babies*.
For over a hundred years this book has been a favorite of the young and young-in-heart. A juvenile classic which can be read over a wide span of years.

Arthur Ransome, *The Fool of the World and the Flying Ship*, ill. by Uri Shulevitz.

Snow White and the Seven Dwarfs, ill. by Nancy E. Burkert.
The old story with medieval-style drawings that make it a collector's item. Published by Farrar, Straus & Giroux.

Hans Christian Anderson, *The Nightingale*, ill. by Nancy E. Burkert.

Ruth A. Sonneborn, *The Lollipop Party*.
A little boy entertains his teacher who comes to call unexpectedly.

Carolyn Haywood, *B Is for Betsy*.
A series on the first year of school for a typical American girl.
_____, *Little Eddie*.
A series on the adventures of a seven-year-old boy.

Jean Berwick, *Arthur and the Golden Guinea*.
Story set in Williamsburg which gives the feel of colonial life in the context of a good tale.

Ruth Craft, *The Fair*, ill. by Pieter Brueghel.
Sections of this exciting, famous painting are blocked off to be examined in detail, complete with appropriate rhymes. Published by Lippincott.

Mary O'Neill, *Hailstones and Halibut Bones*.
Delightful, imaginative poems about color enjoyed by all ages.

Lorraine and Jerrold Beim, *Two Is a Team*.
Story of teamwork and friendship between a little black boy and his white friend.

Alice Dalgliesh, *Ride on the Wind*.
Story of Lindbergh and the "Spirit of St. Louis."

Aldren A. Watson, *Where Everyday Things Come From.*

Tim and Greg Hildebrandt, *How Do They Build It?*

Dale Fife, *What's the Prize, Lincoln?*
An inner city boy guesses the right number of gumdrops in a fishbowl and wins. So he keeps on entering contests! Others in the series are *What's New, Lincoln?* and *Who's in Charge of Lincoln?*

Michael Bond, *A Bear Called Paddington.*
Paddington always manages to live on the edge of disaster and emerge triumphant. A favorite of all children. Look for others in the series.

Richard Kennedy, *Come Again in the Spring.*
Sensitive story about Old Hark who bargains with Death and wins until Spring.

A. A. Milne, *Winnie the Pooh.*
———, *The House at Pooh Corner.*
Every child and adult will enjoy this lovable bear and his friends.

Good Reading II—Grades Four Through Six

A. A. Milne, *Winnie the Pooh.*
———, *The House at Pooh Corner.*
These books get funnier as you get older!

Ingri and Edgar D'Aulaire, *Abraham Lincoln.*
Beautifully written and illustrated life of Lincoln from boyhood through the presidency. Caldecott Medal. Look for other D'Aulaire biographies.

Georgene Faulkner and John Becker, *Melindy's Medal.*
Melindy, a small black girl, moves to a housing project from a basement apartment.

E. B. White, *Charlotte's Web,* ill. by Garth Williams.
A profound, tender story of a pig and a spider. A classic story of friendship.
———, *Stuart Little.*
Story of the exploits of a debonair mouse.

————, *The Trumpet of the Swan.*
Louis, a voiceless trumpeter swan, learns to play a trumpet and finds fame, fortune, and fatherhood.

Laura Ingalls Wilder, *Little House on the Prairie,* ill. by Garth Williams.
First of a series of stories about the Ingalls family, told with skill—full of family warmth and the adventure of pioneer days.
————, *Little House in the Big Woods.*
————, *On the Banks of Plum Creek.*
————, *By the Shores of Silver Lake.*
————, *Little Town on the Prairie.*
————, *The Long Winter.*
————, *These Happy Golden Years.*
————, *Farmer Boy.*
Several of these are available in paperback in a slipcase.

Eleanor Estes, *The Moffats.*
The Moffats—four children and mama—and their friends have lively adventures despite a limited income.
————, *The Middle Moffat.*
Deals with the problem of being a middle child.
————, *Rufus M.*
————, *Ginger Pye.*

Louise Dickinson Rich, *Star Island Boy.*
Eleven-year-old Larry is sent to his latest set of foster parents who live on an island off the coast of Maine where he finds a permanent home.

William Pène du Bois, *The Alligator Case,* ill. by author.
A young boy assumes many disguises as he tracks down villains who disguise themselves as alligators.
————, *Otto and the Magic Potatoes.*
Story of a giant dog who proves himself to be a hero in dealing with a wealthy fanatic who raises roses and potatoes.
————, *The Horse in the Camel Suit.*
————, *The Great Geppy.*
————, *The Giant.*

Natalie S. Carlson, *The Empty Schoolhouse.*
The story of a ten-year-old black girl in a small Louisiana town and her loneliness and abuse as the first to integrate her school.

Beverly Cleary, Henry Huggins.
The hilarious adventure of Henry, his dog Ribsy, and their friends. Look for others in this series.
_____, Ramona the Pest.
A female akin to Henry.
_____, Otis Spofford.
Otis stirs up a little excitement at school. Brimful of humor.
_____, Ellen Tebbits.
About a fourth grader whose life is made miserable by long underwear.
_____, Socks.
Story of a young tabby cat who rules the household until an infant son is born. His triumph over rejection is hilarious and touching.
_____, The Mouse and the Motorcycle.
_____, Runaway Ralph.

Dorothy Canfield Fisher, Understood Betsy.
Timid Elizabeth is sent to live with distant relatives in Vermont. An old, tender story of a child's awakening to self and others.

Ruth S. Gannett, My Father's Dragon, ill. by author.
Humor, wit, and fantasy in the rescue of a benevolent dragon. Also look for Elmer and the Dragon and The Dragons of Blueland.

George Selden, The Cricket in Times Square, ill. by Garth Williams.
A cricket from Connecticut spends the summer in a New York subway station helped by three friends—a boy, a cat, and a fast-talking Broadway mouse.

Ellen MacGregor, Miss Pickerell Goes to Mars.
Precise Miss Pickerell wouldn't go on a Ferris wheel, then suddenly finds herself whisked off to another planet. Interesting adventures in this and others in the series: Miss Pickerell Goes to the Arctic and Miss Pickerell Goes Underseas.

Jane Langton, Her Majesty Grace Jones.
Grace comes to believe she is an heir to the throne, a real princess, but nobody treats her like royalty. Irresistible. Also look for The Boyhood of Grace Jones.

Edward Ormondroyd, *Time at the Top.*
Susan rides on an apartment elevator to a floor that is not there
and finds herself in the year 1881.

Edith Nesbit, *Five Children and It.*
A group of children discover a sand-fairy who both enlivens
and confuses their lives. The following books are more about
the same children.
_____, *The Story of the Treasure Seekers.*
_____, *The Story of the Amulet.*
_____, *The Phoenix and the Carpet.*
_____, *The Railway Children.*
_____, *The Enchanted Castle.*

Mary Norton, *The Borrowers.*
Tiny people, no taller than a pencil, live in old houses and
borrow what they need from whoever lives there.
_____, *The Borrowers Afield.*
_____, *The Borrowers Afloat.*
_____, *The Borrowers Aloft.*

Ruth Sawyer, *Roller Skates.*
A little girl explores New York City on roller skates in the
1890s. Newbery Medal.

Lois Lenski, *Strawberry Girl.*
Story of a little Cracker girl, full of Florida Lake Country
flavor.
_____, *Cotton in My Sack.*
_____, *Judy's Journey.*
_____, *Prairie School.*
_____, *Blue Ridge Billy.*

Richard and Florence Atwater, *Mr. Popper's Penguins.*
Humorous story of a house painter and his pet penguin who
becomes so lonesome that Mr. Popper borrows a penguin
from the zoo. A modern classic.

Betty MacDonald, *Mrs. Piggle-Wiggle*, ill. by Hilary Knight.
Series of stories about a remarkable old lady whom children
love because she lives in an upside-down house and smells of
cookies and was once married to a pirate.

Elizabeth Enright, *Then There Were Five*.
_____, *The Saturdays*.
_____, *Spiderweb for Two*.
_____, *The Four-Story Mistake*.
Marvelous stories of the lively Melendy family and their adventures. Favorites of children.
_____, *Thimble Summer*.
Newbery Medal.
_____, *Gone-Away Lake*.
_____, *Tatsinda*.
A fantasy.

Marguerite De Angeli, *Bright April*, ill. by author.
A modern story about a little black girl in Germantown, Pa.
_____, *Thee, Hannah!*
_____, *The Door in the Wall: Story of Medieval London*.

Carol R. Brink, *Caddie Woodlawn*.
A redheaded tomboy and her brother have exciting encounters with friendly Indians on the Wisconsin frontier. Newbery Medal.
_____, *Andy Buckram's Tin Men*.
Story of a boy who builds four robots which help rescue several people from a flood.

Hugh Lofting, *The Voyages of Dr. Doolittle*.
Wildly impossible and very funny adventures of a doctor who learns animal languages. Look for others in series.

Frances Hodgson Burnett, *The Secret Garden*, ill. by Tasha Tudor.
Three children find a secret garden and make it bloom again; the garden, in turn, changes the children.
_____, *A Little Princess*.

Jean Little, *Mine for Keeps*.
Exceptionally well-handled story of Sally who comes home to live after five years at a cerebral palsy center. Faced with new adjustments, she is helped by her pet dog to win security and friends. *Spring Begins in March* is the sequel.
_____, *From Anna*.
A Jewish family leaves Germany during World War II to start life anew in Canada, where Anna, the youngest of five, is a loner and needs help.

————, *Look Through My Window*.
Emily goes to live with four young cousins and makes a new
friend, Kate, the child of a Jewish-Gentile couple, and together they learn to understand themselves. The story is continued in *Kate*.

Eleanor Clymer, *My Brother Stevie*.
A story true to inner city conditions, movingly told.

Louisa May Alcott, *Little Women*.
Classic story of family love, tragedy, and romance in the lives
of the four March sisters.
————, *Little Men*.
————, *Jo's Boys*.

James Daugherty, *Daniel Boone*.
Biography of a childhood hero. Newbery Medal.

John O'Brien, *Silver Chief: Dog of the North*, ill. by Kurt Wiese.
Classic story of a magnificent dog, part husky and part wolf.

Kenneth Grahame, *The Wind in the Willows*, ill. by Ernest
Shepard.
Beloved Mole, Rat, Badger, and Toad in their classic adven-
tures.
————, *The Reluctant Dragon*.
Tale of a dragon who prefers poetry to battle.

William Pène duBois, *Twenty-One Balloons*.
Adventure of a professor who sails around the world in a
balloon. Newbery Medal.

Monica Shannon, *Dobry*.
Beautifully written story of family life in the mountains of
Bulgaria.

Robert McCloskey, *Homer Price*.
Read the adventures of this boy just for fun.

Esther Shephard, *Paul Bunyan*, ill. by Rockwell Kent.
Legends about the gigantic lumberman of mighty strength.

Johann D. Wyss, *Swiss Family Robinson*.
An adventure of shipwreck and survival that delights every
child.

Anna Sewell, *Black Beauty.*
Moving story of perhaps the most famous horse of all. Don't substitute simplified versions for small children.

Johanna H. Spyri, *Heidi.*
Another classic about a girl, her grandfather, and a boy named Peter, movingly told, set in the Swiss mountains. Don't choose a simplified edition.

James Barrie, *Peter Pan*, ill. by Nora S. Unwin.
Familiar story of a boy who doesn't want to grow up. Read it in the original form for the full impact of the story.

Lewis Carroll, *Alice's Adventures in Wonderland and Through the Looking Glass.*
Absolutely ageless classic of fanciful nonsense and satire. A must for every child—and adults as well.

Frank L. Baum, *The Wizard of Oz.*
The experience of reading this book aloud will be quite different than watching the classic film on television.
_____, *The Lost Princess of Oz.*

George MacDonald, *At the Back of the North Wind.*
Classical fantasy with deep meanings and the adventure of a boy's love for the North Wind.
_____, *The Princess and the Goblin.*
In which a princess and a miner's son outwit the evil mountain goblins. *The Princess and Curdie* is the sequel.
_____, *The Golden Key.*
_____, *The Light Princess.*

Carlo Collodi, *Adventures of Pinocchio.*
An old favorite which has been watered-down with simplified editions.

Eleanor Farjeon, *Martin Pippin in the Apple Orchard.*
Stories of fantasy and nonsense.

Andrew Lang, *Arabian Nights.*
Well-told tales of a romantic faraway.

Howard Pyle, *The Story of Sir Lancelot and His Companions.*
_____, *Some Merry Adventures of Robin Hood.*

Sidney Lanier, *The Boy's King Arthur*, ill. by N. C. Wyeth.

Arthur Rackham, *Cinderella*.

Sydney Taylor, *All-of-a-Kind Family*.
———, *More All-of-a-Kind Family*.
———, *A Papa Like Everyone Else*.
Warm and moving stories of Jewish family life in New York City.

Glen Rounds, *The Blind Colt*, ill. by author.
Born blind, a mustang colt learns to "see" with his ears and nose.
———, *The Day the Circus Came to Lone Tree*.
Hilarious story for any age.
———, *Of Paul, the Mighty Logger*.
Tall tales about Paul Bunyan.
———, *Whitey Ropes and Rides*.
A series about Whitey's adventures as a cowhand.
———, *Hunted Horses*.
Story about the wild horses of the mesa.

Doris Gates, *Little Vic*.
A black stableboy helps Little Vic win the Santa Anita Handicap and breaks down the prejudice of his white trainer.
———, *Blue Willow*.
Story of a girl whose family are migrant workers.
———, *The Cat and Mrs. Cary*.
A woman finds she has a talking cat.

E. L. Konigsburg, *Altogether, One at a Time*.
Collection of four humorous short stories which highlight the emotions and minds of children.
———, *From the Mixed-Up Files of Mrs. Basil E. Frankweiler*.
Two children run away from home and live for days at the Metropolitan Museum of Art. Newbery Medal.
———, *About the B'nai Bagels*, ill. by author.
A member of the B'nai Bagels, a Little League team, has problems. His mother is team manager, his brother is the coach, and he must prepare for his Bar Mitzvah!
———, *Father's Arcane Daughter*.

Astrid Lindgren, *Pippi Longstocking*.
Pippi lives alone except for her monkey, her horse, and her

fortune in gold pieces, but she creates a sensation wherever she goes. Her hilarious adventures are continued in other books in the series.

———, *Pippi Goes on Board.*

———, *Pippi in the South Seas.*

———, *Seacrow Island.*
Engaging story about a Swedish family and an enchanting island.

———, *Mischievous Meg.*

———, *The Children of Noisy Village.*
A series.

———, *Rasmus and the Vagabond.*

Rudyard Kipling, *The Jungle Books.*
Two volumes. Exciting episodes with jungle animals written with powerful imaginative appeal.

———, *Just So Stories.*
For younger children.

Pamela Travers, *Mary Poppins.*
Mary Poppins blew in with the east wind to be nurse for the Banks children.

———, *Mary Poppins Comes Back.*

———, *Mary Poppins Opens the Door.*

———, *Mary Poppins in the Park.*

———, *Friend Monkey.*

Robert Lawson, *Rabbit Hill,* ill. by author.
A good story with good characterizations. Warm and humorous. Newbery Medal.

———, *Tough Winter.*
Its sequel.

———, *Ben and Me.*
About a mouse who lived in Ben Franklin's hat. Delightful.

———, *Mr. Revere and I.*

Eric Knight, *Lassie Come Home.*
Classic dog story every child should know.

Antoine De Saint-Exupery, *The Little Prince.*
After a forced landing in the Sahara, a flier meets the Little Prince of Asteroid B 612.

Jean George, *My Side of the Mountain*.
A contemporary Robinson Crusoe—a small boy learns to survive and live with nature in the Catskills.

Kate Seredy, *The Good Master*.
Story of a Hungarian tomboy who is sent by her father to stay on her uncle's ranch. Beautifully written.
———, *The White Stag*.
———, *The Singing Tree*.
———, *The Chestry Oak*.
———, *A Tree for Peter*.

Dorothy Sterling, *Freedom Train*.
Story of Harriet Tubman, the courageous escaped slave who devoted her life to helping others escape.

Meindert DeJong, *Wheel on the School*, ill. by Maurice Sendak.
Storks are brought back to their island by school children in a Dutch village. Newbery Medal.
———, *The Singing Hill*.
Story of a boy who gains self-confidence through his love for an old horse.
———, *Far Out the Long Canal*.
Two-day adventure of a Dutch boy who learns to skate when he is on a wild adventure where the ice is thin.
———, *The House of Sixty Fathers*.
Dramatic account of a Chinese boy during the Japanese War. An unforgettable emotional experience.
———, *Shadrach*.
Sensitive story of Davie and his black rabbit.
———, *Along Came a Dog*.
———, *Smoke Above the Lane*.
———, *The Last Little Cat*.

Mary Mapes Dodge, *Hans Brinker or The Silver Skates*.
Strong characterization and a complex and exciting plot have kept this book on the list of children's favorites.

Jesse Jackson, *Call Me Charley*.
Realistic, well-written approach to the contemporary racial problem.

Rachael Field, *Hitty—Her First Hundred Years*.
Within the fine story of a New England doll and her experi-

ences is much quaint observation and philosophy. For girls who are beyond the doll age.
_____, *Calico Bush*.
Distinguished colonial story with a well-sustained plot.

Roald Dahl, *Charley and the Chocolate Factory*.
Rollicking fun when Charley wins a trip to the chocolate factory. Full of extremes and humor.
_____, *James and the Giant Peach*.
Zany story of James's adventures inside a giant peach.

Scott O'Dell, *Island of the Blue Dolphins*.
Haunting story, based on fact, of an Indian girl who is forced to spend eighteen years alone on an island off the coast of California. *Zia* is a sequel to it.
_____, *The Black Pearl*.

Dayton O. Hyde, *Cranes in My Corral*.
An Oregon rancher tells of raising four sand-hill cranes.

Mel Ellis, *Flight of the White Wolf*.
A boy and a white wolf flee together in the northern Wisconsin forest. A tough, compassionate story.

Gerald Durrell, *Birds, Beasts and Relatives*.
An owl in the attic, a bear in the parlor, an overweight sister with acne, and an eccentric brother!

Farley Mowat, *Owls in the Family*, ill. by Robert Frankenberg.
The many adventures of a family who adopt two owls.

Walt Morey, *Gentle Ben*.
The lonely son of a salmon fisherman befriends an Alaskan brown bear which has been mistreated.
_____, *Gloomy Gus*.
A bear cub and a lonely boy in Alaska whose father says the pet bear must go.
_____, *Kavik the Wolf Dog*.
_____, *Runaway Stallion*.

James Thurber, *Many Moons*.
A princess wants the moon, and the king orders one person after another to bring it to her. One succeeds.

Marguerite Henry, *King of the Wind*, ill. by Wesley Dennis.
Marguerite Henry is considered by many to be the most successful writer of horse stories. If you like one, you will want to read them all.
———, *Black Gold.*
———, *Born to Trot.*
———, *Misty of Chincoteague.*
———, *Justin Morgan Had a Horse.*
———, *Brighty of the Grand Canyon.*
———, *Sea Star.*
———, *Stormy, Misty's Foal.*
———, *White Stallion of Lipizza.*

Barbara Cohen, *The Carp in the Bathtub.*
Momma keeps a carp swimming in the bathtub just before Passover when she wants to make gefilte fish.

John D. Fitzgerald, *The Great Brain*, ill. by Mercer Mayer.
Lively funny book, skillfully written, about Tom and his great brain. The setting is Mormon, turn-of-the-century Adenville, Utah. Watch for *More Adventures of the Great Brain* and others in the series.

Louise Fitzhugh, *Harriet the Spy.*
Precocious Harriet keeps a secret notebook which she fills with utterly honest jottings about everyone she knows. Delightful. *The Long Secret* is the sequel.

Betsy Byars, *The Summer of the Swans.*
Story of fourteen-year-old Sara and how her life changes when her younger, mentally retarded brother disappears. Newbery Medal.
———, *The Midnight Fox.*
A city boy learns about nature and a black fox which he protects from his uncle's gun.
———, *The Eighteenth Emergency.*
Benjie wins over a bully who threatens him.
———, *The House of Wings.*
Sammy finds himself alone with his grandfather in a dilapidated old house and tries to run away. But the old man's way with a wounded crane wins the boy to a warm friendship.
———, *After the Goat Man.*
———, *The Hundred Dresses.*

Lucretia P. Hale, *The Complete Peterkin Papers*.
A series of amusing incidents from the life of the Peterkin family. A classic.

Esther Forbes, *America's Paul Revere*, ill. by Lynd Ward.
Story about a well-known hero which includes informative background to the Revolutionary War.

Felix Salten, *Bambi: A Life in the Woods*.
A book for ten-year-olds plus, this tender story shows deep respect for the wild creatures of the forest. It is often read too young in a popularized edition.

Walter Farley, *Black Stallion*.
A wild Arabian stallion and the boy who trained him. Look for others in this series.

Arthur Ransome, *Swallows and Amazons*.
A small island creates a great summer adventure for two sets of English children.

Charles and Mary Lamb, *Tales from Shakespeare*.
Introduces children to literature they will later moot.

Armstrong Sperry, *Call It Courage*.
Story of a Polynesian boy's courage in facing the sea he feared. Newbery Medal.

Joseph Krumgold, *Onion John*.
Twelve-year-old Andy's dilemma over social pressure exerted on a simple immigrant vegetable peddler. Newbery Medal.

Anne Holm, *North to Freedom*.
A boy who has grown up in a concentration camp makes his way across Europe alone.

Elizabeth Coatsworth, *John, the Unlucky*.
A young Dane is lost in a snowstorm in Greenland in the late nineteenth century, and a stranger leads him to a secret valley.
———, *The Princess and the Lion*.
———, *The House of the Swan*.

Julie Edwards, Mandy.
    Mandy, a ten-year-old orphan, climbs over the orphanage wall and finds her very own home in a deserted forest.

Andrew Lang, Red Fairy Book.
———, Blue Fairy Book.
———, Yellow Fairy Book.
———, Green Fairy Book.
    For those who like fairy stories.

Norton Juster, The Phantom Tollbooth, ill. by Jules Feiffer.
    A clever book—funny, philosophical, and full of big words. Given a tollbooth, Miles ventures into a fantastic world.

Kate Douglas Wiggin, Rebecca of Sunnybrook Farm.
    Story of a child who lives with two maiden aunts in a New England town. An old favorite too good to miss.

Jean Craighood George, Julie of the Wolves.
    The story of an Eskimo girl who is cared for by Arctic wolves; it teaches about cultural changes in a changing world.

L. M. Montgomery, Anne of Green Gables.
    Millions of young readers have laughed and cried with Anne as she grows from awkward adolescence into beautiful womanhood. Several others in the series, including, Anne of Avonlea and Anne of the Island.

Helen Keller, The Story of My Life.
    Unable to hear or see, Helen Keller discovered the world through her fingertips.

Joan Aiken, The Wolves of Willoughy Chase.
———, Nightbirds on Nantucket.
———, Black Hearts in Battersea.
———, The Whispering Mountain.
    Stories of adventure, romance, and melodrama for junior high students.

Mildred D. Taylor, Roll of Thunder, Hear My Cry.
    Story of a black family's struggle in Mississippi during the Depression. Seen through the eyes of a nine-year-old. Newbery Medal.

Hester Burton, *In Spite of All the Terror.*
Liz Hawkins is evacuated from London during the war. Historically accurate and well-written.

Madeline L'Engle, *A Wrinkle in Time.*
Interplanetary suspense and adventure. Newbery Medal. L'Engle is a fine author with whom your children should become acquainted.
_____, *A Wind in the Door.*
Sequel to above title.
_____, *Dragons in the Waters.*
A family become embroiled in a murder mystery in South America.
_____, *Meet the Austins.*
_____, *The Moon by Night.*
_____, *The Young Unicorns.*
_____, *The Arm of the Starfish.*

John Christopher, *The White Mountains.*
_____, *The City of Gold and Lead.*
_____, *The Pool of Fire.*
A trilogy of compelling science fiction about extraterrestrial invaders threatening to snuff out life on earth.

Lloyd Alexander, *The High King.*
Excellent fantasy, well-written, and based on Welsh legend. A series of stories with substance. Highly recommended.
_____, *The Book of Three.*
_____, *The Black Cauldron.*
_____, *The Castle of Llyr.*
_____, *Taran Wanderer.*
_____, *Coll and His White Pig.*
_____, *The Truthful Harp.*

Walter D. Edmonds, *The Matchlock Gun.*
Exciting true story of a boy who protected his mother and sister from Indians in the Hudson valley. Newbery Medal.

William Faulkner, *The Wishing Tree.*
The only children's story by Faulkner: the tale is about Maurice who sets out to find the Wishing Tree.

C.S. Lewis, *The Narnia Chronicles.*
Seven books, now available in paperback in a slipcase set. Lewis believed that any book worth reading at ten should be

worth reading at fifty, and he wrote that kind. Ageless. Includes: *The Lion, the Witch, and the Wardrobe; Prince Caspian; Voyage of the Dawn Treader; The Silver Chair; The Horse and His Boy; The Magician's Nephew;* and *The Last Battle.*

Good Reading III—Teens and Mature Readers

Mark Twain, *The Adventures of Tom Sawyer.*
_____, *The Adventures of Huckleberry Finn.*
_____, *The Prince and the Pauper.*
_____, *A Connecticut Yankee in King Arthur's Court.*
   Classics too good for any child to miss reading as Twain wrote them.

Scott O'Dell, *The Hawk That Dare Not Hunt by Day.*
   Set in the time of Tyndale's translation of the Bible into English, Tom Barton and his Uncle Jack, a smuggler, are caught up in Tyndale's problems.
_____, *The Dark Canoe.*
_____, *The King's Fifth.*

Ian Fleming, *Chitty-Chitty Bang-Bang.*
   A magical racing car flies, floats, and has a real talent for getting the Pott family in and out of trouble.

Sheila Burnford, *The Incredible Journey.*
   Journey of a Siamese cat, an English bull terrier, and a Labrador retriever.

Jean Merrill, *The Pushcart War.*
   A satirical story of New York's pushcart peddlers who carry on guerrilla war with the traffic-clogging trailer trucks.

Robert Murphy, *The Pond.*
   Story of a boy and a pond, written with great style and feeling about the pangs and pleasures of adolescence.
_____, *Wild Geese Calling.*
   Story of a boy who nurses a wounded Canadian goose and tries to keep him as a companion.

Ann Nolan Clark, *Secret of the Andes.*
   Intriguing story of a young man's discovery of who he is. Newbery Medal.

Judith Kerr, *When Hitler Stole Pink Rabbit.*
Story of a Jewish German refugee family who escaped to Switzerland to avoid Nazi persecution.

Virginia Hamilton, *Arilla Sun Down.*
Arilla, part Indian and part black, is a marvelous character, learning new things about her own identity. Sensitive writing.
_____, *House of Dies Dreer.*
_____, *Zeely.*
_____, *M. C. Higgins, the Great.*

Armstrong Sperry, *Danger to Windward.*
Adventures at sea, from whaling to capture by the Polynesians.
_____, *Thunder Country.*
_____, *Frozen Fire.*

Ernest Gaines, *The Autobiography of Miss Jane Pittman.*
The story of a wise black lady who has great insights into the human condition.

Will James, *Smoky.*
Written in cowboy vernacular, this is a powerful book. If children are going to weep over animal stories, here is one worth their tears. Newbery Medal.

Esther Forbes, *Johnny Tremain.*
A novel for young and old about the American Revolution. Newbery Medal.

Stephen Meader, *Shadow in the Pines.*
Fathers have been known to borrow this thrilling mystery from their sons. Good prose, fast-moving and exciting.
_____, *Who Rides in the Dark?*
_____, *Whaler 'Round the Horn.*
_____, *Clear for Action.*
_____, *The Fish Hawk's Nest.*
_____, *Red Horse Hill.*

Tomas Szabo, *Boy on the Rooftop.*
Story about the Hungarian revolution and escape to the West. Exciting reading, especially for early teens who read with difficulty.

Rumer Godden, *An Episode of Sparrows.*
Sentimental, touching, yet amusing story of two waifs living in a section of bombed-out London who effect profound changes in the lives of their neighbors.

Betty Byars, *Trouble River.*
To escape from Indians, a boy and his grandmother travel forty miles down Trouble River on a homemade raft.

William O. Steele, *Winter Danger.*
No writer for children today re-creates wilderness life more vividly or movingly.
——, *Flaming Arrows.*
Story of Tennessee settlers protecting themselves against raiding Indians.
——, *The Lone Hunt.*
Story of a buffalo hunt and a boy's struggle to grow up.

Jules Verne, *Around the World in Eighty Days.*
——, *Journey to the Center of the Earth.*
——, *20,000 Leagues Under the Sea.*

Elizabeth George Speare, *The Bronze Bow.*
Daniel's hatred of the Romans is turned to love by Jesus of Nazareth.
——, *Calico Captive.*
——, *The Witch of Blackbird Pond.*
Historical romance set in Puritan Connecticut with a theme of witchcraft. Newbery Medal.

Jean Lee Latham, *Carry On, Mr. Bowditch.*
Fictionalized biography about an exciting historical figure of the 1770s. Newbery Medal.

Marjorie Rawlings, *The Yearling,* ill. by N. C. Wyeth.
Written for adults, but appropriated by children. A beautifully written story of a lonely boy. Be sure to find the edition with Wyeth's superb illustrations.

Robert Louis Stevenson, *Treasure Island.*
——, *Kidnapped,* ill. by N. C. Wyeth.
——, *Strange Case of Dr. Jekyll and Mr. Hyde.*
——, *The Black Arrow.*
Good writing, exciting plots—who could ask for more!

Fred Gipson, *Old Yeller*.
Story of a fourteen-year-old boy and the ugly stray dog he came to love.

Jack London, *Call of the Wild*.
Adventure in the frozen northlands—a classic.

James A. Kjelgaard, *Big Red*.
Champion Irish setter and a trapper's son have exciting adventures together.
_____, *Irish Red: Son of Big Red*.
_____, *Outlaw Red*.
_____, *Haunt Fox*.
_____, *Lion Hound*.
_____, *Trailing Trouble*.

Mary O'Hara, *My Friend Flicka*.
A boy, his mother, and a pony on a western ranch—a story which Americans young and old have taken to their hearts.

John Steinbeck, *The Red Pony*.
When his pony dies, John discovers meaning to life.

Sterling North, *Rascal*.
Autobiographical account of the beauty of nature as experienced by an eleven-year-old and his pet raccoon.
_____, *So Dear to My Heart*.

T. H. White, *The Sword in the Stone*.
Humorous fantasy about the adventures of the boy who became King Arthur.

Eric P. Kelly, *The Trumpeter of Krakow*.
Story of tense political intrigue in fifteenth century Poland. Newbery Medal.

Rudyard Kipling, *Captains Courageous*.
A sea adventure about a spoiled American child who becomes a man, displaying Kipling's skill in writing.
_____, *Kim*.

Nathaniel Benchley, *A Necessary End*.
Story of a ship and its crew. A good writer.

_____, *Bright Candles*.
Story of a sixteen-year-old boy in the Dutch Resistance during World War II.
_____, *Only Earth and Sky Last Forever*.
Dark Elk joins Crazy Horse at the Battle of the Little Big Horn.
_____, *Gone and Back*.
Seven-year odyssey of a family in the 1880s.

D. R. Sherman, *The Lion's Paw*.
Pxui frees an awesome wounded lion from a trap and, contrary to custom, does not kill him to show his manliness. He has to defend his unorthodox behavior and accept the responsibility for his act. "One of the best books I've read in a long, long time," said one high schooler.

Daniel Defoe, *Robinson Crusoe*, ill. by N. C. Wyeth.
Read the unabridged editon of this story of a shipwrecked man.

Jesse Jackson, *Tessie*.
Story of the conflicts that beset a Harlem teen-ager as she tries to reconcile two different worlds.

Sir Arthur Conan Doyle, *Adventures of Sherlock Holmes*.
_____, *Hound of the Baskervilles*.
In Sherlock Holmes, Doyle has created a character so real that many think he actually lived.

John Buchan, *Adventures of Richard Hannay*.
A trilogy of spy stories, gripping, well-written, and hard to put down. Skillful weaving of plot.

G. K. Chesterton, *Father Brown Mystery Stories*.
At last the clever sleuthing of Father Brown has returned to print! A most unorthodox detective. Several books in the series.

James Thurber, *The Thirteen Clocks*.
If you haven't met James Thurber's sophisticated and serious humor, this is a good place to begin. You'll love it.

Charlotte Bronte, *Jane Eyre*.

Emily Bronte, *Wuthering Heights*.
The Bronte sisters spin quite different tales, both of which have remained popular through the years.

Irene Hunt, *Up a Road Slowly*.
Talented and motherless, Julie tells of her growing years into high school. Reflective, excellent writing, good for certain kinds of girls. Newbery Medal.
_____, *Across Five Aprils*.

James Hilton, *Good-bye, Mr. Chips*.
Moving portrait of an English schoolmaster and his three generations of boys.
_____, *Lost Horizon*.

Joy Adamson, *Born Free*.
A lioness raised among people is retrained for jungle life.

Frank Gilbreth and Ernestine Carey, *Cheaper by the Dozen*.
Hilarious adventures of a family brought up in a house where father is an industrial efficiency expert.

Willian Henry Hudson, *Green Mansions*.
Romantic old favorite written in 1904.
_____, *A Little Boy Lost*.

Jessamyn West, *Cress Delahanty*.
Story of a girl who grows up on a California ranch.
_____, *The Massacre at Fall Creek*.
Story of the brutal killing of a group of Indians and the subsequent pursuit of justice.

Kenneth Roberts, *Northwest Passage*.
Exciting story of a search for the passage to the Northwest.
_____, *Rabble in Arms*.
A story of the American Revolution by a good writer.

Stephen Crane, *The Red Badge of Courage*.
A soldier in the Civil War writes dramatically of his experiences.

Washington Irving, *The Legend of Sleepy Hollow*.
Story of Ichabod Crane and the Headless Horseman.

Thor Heyerdahl, *Kon-Tiki*.
Exciting account of a voyage across the Pacific on a balsa raft.

Charles Dickens, *David Copperfield*.
_____, *Oliver Twist*.
_____, *A Tale of Two Cities*.
_____, *Great Expectations*.
Children will meet people in these books whom they will never forget and will come to understand something of the history of the times.

O. E. Rolvaag, *Giants in the Earth*.
Saga of a Norwegian immigrant family in South Dakota in pioneering days.

Willa Cather, *My Antonia*.
A superb writer tells the story of an immigrant girl growing up in America.

Richard Llewellyn, *How Green Was My Valley*.
Beautifully written novel of Welsh mining villagers.

Lloyd C. Douglas, *The Robe*.
After the Crucifixion, a Roman soldier wins Christ's robe and is never the same again.

Leo Tolstoy, *Anna Karenina*.
A classic translated from the Russian which mature readers will enjoy.

Alexander Dumas, *The Three Musketeers*.
Story of three swordsmen who serve the king—an exciting adventure of their great feat in saving King Louis XIII from Richelieu's plot.

Victor Hugo, *Les Miserables*.
Story of ex-convict Jean Valjean and his valiant struggle to redeem his past—a commentary on post-Napoleonic France, an adventure story, and a spine-tingling drama.

Lew Wallace, *Ben Hur*.
Exciting historical novel involving the life of Christ.

Richard D. Blackmore, *Lorna Doone*.
Seventeenth century England is the setting for the romance of John Ridd and Lorna of the outlaw Doones.

Marion Anderson, *My Lord, What a Morning*.
Poignant life story of this magnificent singer and human being.

Frances Gray Patton, *Good Morning, Miss Dove*.
A tart and dearly loved schoolteacher affects everyone in the little town where she teaches.

Hal Dorland, *Country Editor's Boy*.
Well-written reminiscences of three years of adolescence in Colorado.

Janet Hickman, *The Valley of the Shadow*.
A superb book based on actual history and characters. Moravian missionaries, living among the Indians, teach resistance to war and bloodshed, and both groups are caught in a tale of deprivation and terror as other white settlers fight to take over the territory.

Conrad Richter, *The Light in the Forest*.
Authentic and understanding picture of Indian and white man relations in the thrilling story of a boy's love for his Indian foster-family.

Charles Kingsley, *Westward Ho!*
Sea adventure in the days of Queen Elizabeth I.

Alan Paton, *Cry, the Beloved Country*.
Moving and haunting story of race relations in South Africa.

Harper Lee, *To Kill a Mockingbird*.
Beautifully written story of two white children in a small Alabama town and of their lawyer father's defense of a black man.

J. R. R. Tolkien, *The Hobbit*.
_____, *The Lord of the Rings* (a trilogy).
Tolkien is a superb storyteller. He creates whole new worlds, peoples them, gives them a language and a history, and takes his readers captive, young and old alike, into his adventures.

Herman Melville, *Moby Dick*.
An epic saga of the one-legged Captain Ahab who swears revenge on the white whale who crippled him.

Alexander Dumas, *Count of Monte Cristo*.
Famous story of adventure, well-worth reading in the original novel.

James Fenimore Cooper, *The Deerslayer*, ill. by N. C. Wyeth.
————, *Last of the Mohicans*.
Superb and lasting adventure stories.

Dee Brown, *Bury My Heart at Wounded Knee*.
A thirty-year history of the expansion of the West from the point of view of the Indian people who lived there.

Elizabeth Janeway, *Ivanov Seven*.
Though he appears doltish, Ivanov of Old Russia attracts every kind of villainous attention, but always comes out triumphant.

Howard Pyle, *Otto of the Silver Hand*.
Life in feudal Germany with robber barons and peaceful monks; the story of the kidnapped son of a robber baron.

Esther Hautzig, *The Endless Steppe: Growing Up in Siberia*.
A warm, personal narrative about the author's family after they were shipped from Poland by cattle car to become laborers in Siberia.

John F. Kennedy, *Profiles in Courage*.
Stories of Americans who took courageous stands on important issues.

Hannah Green, *I Never Promised You a Rose Garden*.
An extraordinary account of a teen-ager's battle with mental illness and the three years she spent fighting for freedom from her self-created prison of fantasy.

Joanne Greenberg, *In This Sign*.
Written by the author of the above book, this often heartbreaking story of those who cannot hear becomes part of the reader's experience.

Fynn, *Mister God, This Is Anna.*
Fynn finds Anna when she is four years old and takes her back
to his mother's home, and from that moment their lives are
filled with delight and discovery, for Anna has a special way
of seeing life.

Sir Walter Scott, *Ivanhoe.*
A novel full of adventure, romantic characters, and suspense.
Story of a noble young Englishman who lived in the time of
Richard the Lion-Hearted.

Joseph Conrad, *Lord Jim.*
One of Conrad's most famous stories of life at sea. Underneath
the excitement is a profound comment on the nature of man.

Thornton Wilder, *Bridge of San Luis Rey.*
A Pulitzer Prize winner, this is a story in which the characters
are brought together in a common catastrophe and their lives
thus interwoven.

Ernest Hemingway, *The Old Man and the Sea.*
Pulitzer-winning story of an old fisherman who, after a siege
of bad luck, hooks the biggest fish he has ever seen.

James Herriot, *All Creatures Great and Small.*
———, *All Things Bright and Beautiful.*
Hilarious, heart-warming, true story of a country veterinarian
whose unique courage and humor have captured his readers.

Michael Crichton, *The Andromeda Strain.*
Four scientists race against the clock to isolate a deadly
microorganism from outer space.

Margaret Craven, *I Heard the Owl Call My Name.*
Moving story of the wisdom and insight a young minister
gained in the last year of his life from his parish in Alaska.

Leonard Mosley, *Lindbergh.*
Penetrating portrait of a great human being whose career
spanned fifty of the nation's most turbulent years. First man to
fly the Atlantic.

Richard Adams, *Watership Down.*
Marvelous adventure of a community of rabbits, complete

with power struggles, the conflict between good and evil. Excellent reading.

————, *Shardik.*

William Morris, *The Well at the World's End.*
————, *Wood Beyond the World.*
Two excellent fantasies by a man who inspired C. S. Lewis to write fantasy.

C. S. Lewis, *Out of the Silent Planet.*
————, *Perelandra.*
————, *That Hideous Strength.*
Three marvelous fantasies for grown-ups that can be read and reread many times.
————, *That Dark Tower and Other Stories.*
Stories found unpublished among Lewis's papers after his death. Will delight his readers.

Charles Williams, *Descent into Hell.*
————, *Many Dimensions.*
————, *The Place of the Lion.*
————, *Shadows of Ecstasy.*
————, *War in Heaven.*
For readers who like myth, mystery, and supernatural implications, these are superb reading—a strange revealing of great truths.

Ursula K. LeGuin, *A Wizard of Earthsea.*
————, *The Tombs of Atuan.*
————, *The Farthest Shore.*
Trilogy of fantasy that is outstanding in wisdom, originality, unforgettable situations, and compelling adventures in the destruction of evil and the triumph of good.

Aleksandr Solzhenitsyn, *The Gulag Archipelago.*
A literary investigation of political policies in U.S.S.R. Excellent.
————, *One Day in the Life of Ivan Denisovich.*
————, *The First Circle.*
————, *For the Good of the Cause.*
————, *The Cancer Ward.*
————, *August 1914.*

Chaim Potok, *The Chosen.*
_____, *The Promise.*
_____, *My Name Is Asher Lev.*
_____, *In the Beginning.*
    Potok is a superb writer. He gets the reader right inside the skin of his Jewish characters, revealing the rich texture of their lives and beliefs.

Poetry Is for Pleasure

Margaret Wise Brown, *Where Have You Been?,* ill. by Barbara Cooney.
_____, *Nibble, Nibble,* ill. by Leonard Weisgard.

Martha Alexander, *Poems and Prayers for the Very Young.*

Aileen Fisher, *Cricket in a Thicket,* ill. by Feodor Rojankovsky.
_____, *But Ostriches,* ill. by Peter Narnall.
_____, *Listen, Rabbit,* ill. by Symeon Shimin.
_____, *Listen, Mouse.*
_____, *In the Middle of the Night,* ill. by Adrienne Adams.
_____, *Feathered Ones and Furry,* ill. by Eric Carle.
_____, *Going Barefoot,* ill. by Adrienne Adams.

Wilma McFarland, *For a Child.*

Blanche Thompson, *All the Silver Pennies.*

Wallace Tripp, *A Great Big Ugly Man Came Up and Tied His Horse to Me: A Book of Nonsense Verse.*
_____, *Granfa' Grig Had a Pig and Other Rhymes Without Reason from Mother Gocse.*

Phyllis McGinly, *All Around the Town,* ill. by Helen Stone.

Beatrice De Regniers, *Poems Children Will Sit Still For.*

Josette Frank, *Poems to Read to the Very Young,* ill. by Dagmar Wilson.

A. A. Milne, *When We Were Very Young.*
_____, *Now We Are Six.*

Edward Lear, *The Complete Nonsense Book.*
—— and Ogden Nash, *The Scroobious Pip*, ill. by Nancy E. Burkert.

Sara Teasdale, *Stars Tonight.*

Rachel Fields, *Taxis and Toadstools.*

Robert Louis Stevenson, *A Child's Garden of Verses.*

Kate Greenaway, *Under the Window.*

Eleanor Farjeon, *Poems for Children.*

Eleanor Doan, *A Child's Treasury of Verse*, ill. by Nancy Munger.

Mary O'Neill, *People I'd Like to Keep*, ill. by Leonard Weisgard.
——, *Hailstones and Halibut Bones.*

Nikki Giovanni, *Spin a Soft Black Song*, ill. by Charles Bible.

William Blake, *Songs of Innocence.*

Henry W. Longfellow, *The Children's Own Longfellow.*

Lillian Moore, *I Feel the Same Way.*

Langston Hughes, *Don't Turn Your Back*, ill. by Grifalconi.

John Ciardi, *The Reason for the Pelican.*
——, *The Man Who Sang the Sillies.*
——, *You Read to Me, I'll Read to You.*
——, *Fast and Slow.*

Ann McGovern, *Arrow Book of Poetry.*

X. J. Kennedy, *One Winter Night in August.*

Robert Frost, *You Come Too.*

Carl Sandburg, *Wind Song.*
——, *Early Moon*, ill. by James Daugherty.

Luci Shaw, *Listen to the Green.*
_____, *The Secret Trees.*

Nancy Larrick, *Piping Down the Valleys Wild,* ill. by Ellen Raskin.

Herbert Read, *This Way, Delight.*

Edward Blishen, *Oxford Book of Poetry for Children.*

Louis Untermeyer, *This Singing World.*

Gladys Adshead and Annis Duff, *Inheritance of Poetry,* ill. by Nora Unwin.

Edward Hodnett, *Poems to Read Aloud.*

L. S. Gannett, *The Family Book of Verse.*

Calvin Miller, *The Singer.*
_____, *The Song.*

Christmas Books To Enjoy

Palmer Brown, *Something for Christmas.*
   Christmas is about *love.*

Rebecca Caudill, *A Certain Small Shepherd.*
   A Christmas miracle allows a little boy to speak for the first time.

Aline Cunningham, *Christmas Is a Birthday.*
   A lovely book for the youngest child.

Marguerite De Angeli, *The Lion in the Box.*
   A special Christmas for a fatherless family.

Masahiro Kasuya, *The Way Christmas Came.*
   Beautiful illustrations and simple text for very young children.

Ezra Jack Keats, *Little Drummer Boy*.

Tasha Tudor, *Take Joy*.
A treasury of Christmas ideas, songs, and literature.

Mae VanderBoom, *The Shepherd's Boy*.
A Jewish shepherd hears the angels' message and later realizes Christ's birth is for everyone.

Carol Woodard, *The Very Special Baby*.
Good picture book for very young children.

Joan Walsh Anglund, *Christmas Is a Time of Giving*.
A small book with warm thoughts.

Edna Miller, *Mousekin's Christmas Eve*.

Patricia Scarry, *The Sweet Smell of Christmas*.
The best of the scratch and sniff books.

Dorothy Van Woerkom, *Journey to Bethlehem*.
The Christmas story told in more detail for middle elementary children.

Adapted by Roz Abisch, *'Twas the Moon of Wintertime*.
The first American Christmas carol.

Robert Barry, *Mr. Willowby's Christmas Tree*.
A delightful book about the strange sharing of a Christmas tree, done in poetry. All ages.

David Budhill, *Christmas Tree Farm*, ill. by Donald Carrick.
The illustrations depict the poetry of nature and the story line gives the story of Christmas.

Kate Douglas Wiggin, *The Birds' Christmas Carol*.
A charming old-fashioned story with a welcome message of love and good-will.

Clement C. Moore, *The Night Before Christmas*, ill. by Arthur Rackham.

Jessie Orton Jones, *Small Rain*, ill. by Elizabeth Orton Jones.
Bible verses, beautifully illustrated.

Dr. Seuss, *How the Grinch Stole Christmas!*

Barbara Robinson, *Best Christmas Pageant Ever.*
A humorous story for fourth-through-sixth grade readers which teaches a good lesson in values.

Ruth Hershey Irwin, *The Christmas Cookie Tree.*
Full of the warm good feeling and smell of Pennsylvania Dutch country, without excessive sentimentality.

Gian-Carlo Menotti, adapted by Frances Frost, *Amahl and the Night Visitors*, ill. by Roger Duvoisin.
Beautiful pictures illustrate the opera story of a crippled boy, the three wise men, and a miracle.

O. Henry. *The Gift of the Magi.*
The simplicity and beauty of the love of two people at Christmas time.

Paul Engle, *An Old-Fashioned Christmas.*
An Iowa Christmas and all the memories of family, smells, and tastes. Full of nostalgia.

Chad Walsh, *Garlands for Christmas.*
A collection of Christmas poems selected by Walsh.

Charles Dickens, *Christmas Stories.*
A collection of twenty-one stories about Christmas.

Leon Morris, *The Story of the Christ Child.*
A devotional study of the nativity stories in Luke and Matthew.

Helping Preschoolers Through Third Graders Grow as Christians

Jerry Vajda, *God Gave Me This Happy Day.*
———, *God Gave Me Toys.*
First books for tiny children. Durable.

Martha Hook, *Little Ones Listen to God*, ill. by Tinka Boren.
Simple one-page Bible stories for tiny children.

Tasha Tudor, *And It Was So.*
Bible verses illustrated in Tudor's lovely style.

Joan Walsh Anglund, *A Book of Good Tidings.*
Fourteen favorite Bible verses illustrated in color by a well-known illustrator.

Sister Shigeko Yano, *As Jesus Grew.*
Beautiful art. The text is about Jesus as a little boy, written originally in Japanese. Rather a homey look at His boyhood.

The Life of Jesus, ill. by Napoli.
Lovely illustrations along with stories from the Gospels. Published by Augsburg.

A. C. Mueller, *My Good Shepherd Bible Story Book*, ill. by Richard Hook.
Excellent Bible story book for young children.

Rachel Field, *Prayer for a Child*, ill. by E. Jones.
Prayer expressing faith, hope, love. Caldecott Medal.

J. Latourette, *The House on the Rock.*

M. Warren, *The Little Boat That Almost Sank.*
_____, *The Great Surprise.*

J. Kramer, *The Baby Born in a Stable.*
The above four and many others are in the Arch Books series, published by Concordia. Short, active stories, taken from the Bible, with colorful contemporary art.

Joanne Marxhaussen, *3 in 1.*
Colorful explanation of the Trinity.
_____, *Thank God for Circles.*
Creatively discusses the concept of God and eternity.

Gerrard A. Pottebaum, *99 Plus One.*
Retelling of the parable of the lost sheep in contemporary form and art.

Mildred Krentel, *I See Four.*
Story of the three men in the fiery furnace.
_____, *Two by Two.*
Story of Noah's ark. Both are charmingly told.

Moments With God, Prayers for Children.
Especially appealing to children because of the colorful photographs and the realistic language of the prayers. Published by Regina Press.

Discovering in God's World.
A series of four books with text and photographs, reminding the reader that the wonderful things in the world were created by God. Published by Regal.

Eileen Lomaskey, *My Book of the Lord's Prayer.*
Good teaching for young children on the meaning of the Lord's Prayer.

Audrey Tarrant, *Barley Loaves and Fishes.*
Beautifully illustrated, the story is told from the point of view of the small boy.

Florence P. Heide, *Who Needs Me?*
_____, *You and Me.*
_____, *God and Me.*
Basic concepts about God, self, and each other. Well-done.

V. Gilbert Beers, *Learning to Read From the Bible Primers.*
_____, *Learning to Read From the Bible Readers.*
Bible stories told with a controlled vocabulary so that children can learn from the Bible as they learn to read. Four books in each series.

Clyde R. Bulla, *Jonah and the Great Fish,* ill. by Helga Aichinger.
_____, *Joseph the Dreamer,* ill. by Gordon Laite.
Beautifully illustrated books of quality, retelling two familiar stories.

Dena Korfker, *Can You Tell Me?*
Answers to questions children ask.

Sheri Haan, *Good News for Children.*
Easily understood and well-organized.

Ethel Barrett, *It Didn't Just Happen.*
An introductory paragraph before each story ties the Bible story to the present.

John Calvin Reid, *Bird Life in Wington.*
Fifty birds take on intriguing characters to teach Christian lessons.
———, *Parables from Nature.*

E, Margaret Clarkson, *Susie's Babies.*
A classroom experience in raising hamsters helps present the facts of procreation in story form. Very well presented.

Helping Third Through Sixth Graders Grow as Christians.

Marian M. Schoolland, *Leading Little Ones to God.*
A wide range of material covered, interesting and basic.

H. S. Vigeveno, *Climbing Up the Mountain.*
Getting the message of the Sermon on the Mount across to children.

Derek Prime, *Tell Me About the Bible, About God.*
———, *Tell Me About the Lord Jesus Christ.*
———, *Tell Me About the Holy Spirit, About the Church.*
———, *Tell Me About the Lord's Prayer.*
Well-done books designed to lend enjoyment to learning basic truths.

Jahsmann and Simon, *Little Visits with God.*
———, *More Little Visits with God.*
Family favorites. Interesting, relevant stories which teach biblical lessons.

Kenneth Taylor, *Devotions for the Children's Hour.*
Doctrinal teaching in many forms, with questions at the end of each chapter for family participation.

Jesse L. Hurlbut, *Hurlbut's Story of the Bible.*
Elsie E. Egermeier, *Egermeier's Bible Story Book.*
Catherine F. Vos, *Child's Story Bible.*
Kenneth N. Taylor, *Taylor's Bible Story Book.*
You will want to have at least one of these to give your child a comprehensive view of the Bible.

Helen L. Taylor, *Little Pilgrim's Progress.*
Simplified version of the famous Bunyan classic which captures the essence of its spiritual truths without writing "down" to children.

George MacDonald, *At the Back of the North Wind.*
_____, *The Princess and the Goblin.*
_____, *The Princess and Curdie.*
_____, *The Light Princess.*
_____, *The Golden Key.*
Written by the man who influenced C. S. Lewis and J. R. R. Tolkien, these books have a touch of the supernatural, much wisdom, and reflect the quality of the author's life and his other writings for adults.

Louise A. Vernon, *The Secret Church.*
Three children witness the persecution and struggle of early Anabaptists (now Mennonites). Fictionalized approach to history. Also look for *Strangers in the Land* (story of the Huguenots) and *The Bible Smuggler* (story of Bible translator William Tyndale).

C. S. Lewis, *The Narnia Chronicles.*
These seven books are first in any class—superb storytelling, beautiful allegories, ageless interest. Mature six-year-olds can listen, and adults won't want to stop with just one chapter!

Paul White, *Jungle Doctor Series.*
Like Aesop, missionary doctor Paul White uses animals to teach Christian truths and give delightful reading. Told with the skill and flavor of a master African storyteller, these books appeal to all ages. Among the many titles in the series are: *Jungle Doctor Operates, Jungle Doctor Attacks Witchcraft, Jungle Doctor Meets a Lion, Jungle Doctor's Fables, Jungle Doctor's Monkey Tales.*

Patricia St. John, *Star of Light*.
>As a missionary in North Africa, the author writes with understanding of the Muslim culture in Morocco. Should be read by adults as well as children.

———, *Three Go Searching*.

———, *Tanglewood Secrets*.

———, *Treasures of the Snow*.

———, *Twice Freed*.
>The story of Onesimus and Philemon. Children love St. John's tender, adventuresome tales. Excellent books, well-written.

Nancy Stone, *Whistle Up the Bay*.
>Three sons of a Swiss immigrant are orphaned in 1870 in a small community in Northern Michigan—a true story of adventure, faith, and initiative.

Joyce Blackburn, *Wilfred Grenfell*.
>Biography of the man who explored Labrador, a man whose adventures stemmed from his inner compulsion to discover and explore for God. Look for other biographies by this author.

Henry Treece, *The Children's Crusade*.
>Exciting, fictionalized account of a strange historical event.

Eugenia Price, *Find Out for Yourself*.
>Encourages young people to think for themselves by facing up to the basic choices in life.

Rosalind Rinker, *The Years That Count*.
>Down-to-earth sharing about understanding self and Jesus Christ.

W. Hoving, *Tiffany's Table Manners for Teen-Agers*.
>Chairman of the Board of the world-famous New York store presents good table manners for young Americans.

Kenneth Taylor, *Almost Twelve*.
>Simple but complete description of God's means for human reproduction.

Helping Teens and Mature Readers
Grow As Christians

Fritz Ridenour, *Who Says?*
What's the truth about the existence of God, the trustworthiness of the Bible, science, and the Christian faith? In a scholarly, popularized style, this book tackles hard questions teen-agers ask, with additional references for those who wish to dig deeper.

Chuck Miller, *Now That I'm A Christian.*
The difference it makes to believe.

I Wish I Had Known.
Thirteen people from various walks of life relate their hang-ups about Christianity and share what they wish they had understood earlier. Published by Zondervan.

Rosalind Rinker, *Prayer: Conversing With God.*
Practical and helpful. Prayer is not making speeches to God.

Ethel Barrett, *Sometimes I Feel Like a Blob.*
Short practical chapters on teen-age life, written especially for Christians.

Fritz Ridenour, *How to Be a Christian Without Being Religious.*
The Book of Romans from Living Bible paraphrase, combined with cleverly illustrated contemporary comments. Excellent for teen-agers.

Barbara Jurgensen, *Men Who Dared.*
Modern retelling of the exciting lives of Bible prophets (including text from Living Bible). An excellent, thoroughly enjoyable introduction to a section of the Bible most teen-agers consider irrelevant.

Johnny Cash, *Man in Black.*
Johnny Cash tells the story of his climb to fame as a singer and his conversion to Jesus Christ.

Corrie Ten Boom/John Sherrill, *The Hiding Place.*
The story of the deliverance of a great woman of faith from a Nazi prison camp, and His sustaining power in her life.

Joni Eareckson, *Joni.*
The unforgettable inspiring story of a young woman's struggle with quadriplegia and depression.

Norman Vincent Peale, *Bible Stories.*
The message of the Bible condensed and simplified. Very readable and good for an adult who is new to the Bible.

Margaret Clarkson, *Conversations with a Barred Owl.*
Delightfully observant of both the ways of birds and the ways of God. Good for bird-watchers.

John Bunyan, *Pilgrim's Progress.*
A fresh edition of an old classic which every Christian should read because of the realistic picture of the Christian life given in it. An enthusiastic foreword by Dr. Frank E. Gaebelein underscores the book's value to today's reader. Published by Zondervan.
———, abridged by Mary Godolphin, *Pilgrim's Progress*, ill. by Robert Lawson.
A beautifully done, simpler-to-read, yet authentic version of John Bunyan's great story.

J. C. Pollock, *Hudson Taylor and Maria.*
An outstanding biography of a real man who was also a great man of God and a missionary pioneer. Highly recommended.

Peter Marshall, *John Doe, Disciple.*
"Sermons for young people" is not a description which does justice to the fine prose, the inspiring thought, and the pull of these sermons by Peter Marshall.

Charles W. Shedd, *Letters to Karen.*
Letters of wisdom to a daughter about life; this book has been popular in all circles.
———, *Letters to Philip.*
Letters to a son on how a woman should be treated.

J. B. Phillips, *Your God Is Too Small.*
Is your God old-fashioned, like a sneaky policeman? Every teen-ager ought to reexamine his idea of God with Phillips.

Oliver Barclay, *Guidance.*
An excellent answer to the question: "How can I know God's will?"

Paul Little, *How to Give Away Your Faith.*
Clues—humorous, practical, and biblical—to sharing your faith with others.

C. S. Lewis, *Mere Christianity.*
With friendly informality, but with his piercing thoroughness, Lewis zeroes in on what he sees as the essentials in Christianity.
———, *The Screwtape Letters.*
Letters from a senior satanic majesty to Wormwood, a junior devil on earth, which cleverly pierce our Christian facade.

Charles Sheldon, *In His Steps.*
An old classic, dramatic and sentimental, but one which still influences young people on the question of priority.

Isobel Kuhn, *By Searching.*
Vital account of a young person's search for God—realistic and well-written.

Mrs. Howard Taylor, *Borden of Yale.*
The biography of a young man and the impact of God's character in his life.

Joe Bayly, *The Gospel Blimp.*
Exaggerated satire on an attempt to evangelize a city with a blimp. Delightful reading, full of barbs which get some important truths across.

David Wilkerson, *The Cross and the Switchblade.*

Grace Irwin, *Least of All Saints.*
———, *Andrew Connington.*
Two excellent novels by a favorite Canadian author, thoroughly Christian, realistic, and well-written.
———, *Servant of Slaves.*
A biographical novel of the life of John Newton, beautifully written; traces his life from slave-trading days to his influential ministry in later years. Highly recommended.

Catherine Marshall, *Christy.*
A moving best-seller about a young woman who goes to teach in the Smoky Mountains and how she comes to love the mountain people.
———, *A Man Called Peter.*
Stirring biography of a famous Scottish preacher, a man who became chaplain to the Senate.

Elisabeth Elliott, *Through Gates of Splendor.*
The story of five missionaries who tried to reach the stone-age Aucas of Ecuador and of their martyrdom.

Russell Hitt, *Jungle Pilot.*
Biography of Nate Saint who flew the jungles of South America; he was one of the men martyred by the Auca Indians.

Ethel Wallis, *The Dayuma Story.*
The gripping sequel to the Auca incident; when two women missionaries return with an Auca girl to this remote tribe.

Ernest Gordon, *Through the Valley of the Kwai.*
The bridge over the Kwai was built in less than two months by starved, exhausted prisoners. This is the story of a demonstration of Christian faith and the difference it made.

William J. Peterson, *Another Hand on Mine.*
A well-written, stirring story of Dr. Carl Becker, missionary to Africa. Highly recommended.

Herman Wouk, *This Is My God.*
A famous contemporary author gives an absorbing statement of his personal faith—an interesting look at Judaism.

John Hercus, *Out of the Miry Clay.*
The story of how God molded David into a faithful servant.

C. S. Lewis, *Out of the Silent Planet.*
———, *Perelandra.*
———, *That Hideous Strength.*
Fantasy at its best; well-worth discussing with someone else to explore the deeper truths of the stories.

Walter Trobisch, *I Loved a Girl.*
A private correspondence between two young Africans and their pastor on sex and love. Enormous appeal.
_____, *I Married You*
The story of two Africans who are working out personal problems, with fresh insights into what marriage is all about.
_____, *Love is a Feeling to be Learned.*
_____, *My Beautiful Feeling: Letters to Ilona.*
_____, *Love Yourself: Self-Acceptance and Depression.*

Dwight Small, *Design for Christian Marriage.*

Herbert J. Miles, *Sexual Understanding Before Marriage.*

HIS Guide to Sex, Singleness and Marriage.
A collection of articles from *HIS* magazine on these subjects. Published by Inter-Varsity Press.

Evelyn M. Duvall, *Why Wait Till Marriage.*
This book builds a strong case for chastity, refuting arguments normally used to justify premarital sex. Also look for her *Love and the Facts of Life.*

Josh McDowell, *More Than a Carpenter.*
Good discussion on who Jesus really is for high school and college students.

Fritz Ridenour, *So, What's the Difference.*
A comparison of Christianity with major religions and cults.

Paul Little, *Know Why You Believe.*
Thoughtful answers to some difficult questions. A book for a thinking young person.
_____, *Know What You Believe.*
_____, *Affirming the Will of God.*

John White, *The Fight: A Practical Handbook for Christian Living.*
Joy and triumph through disciplined Christian commitment.
_____, *Eros Defiled: The Christian and Sexual Sin.*

Quiet Time.
A brief but ever-so-helpful guide to meaningful daily communion with God. Needs to be read often for fresh insights. Published by Inter-Varsity Press.

Michael Griffiths, *Unsplitting Your Christian Life.*
Practical Christian living. Good reading for high school and college students.

Masumi Toyotome, *Three Kinds of Love.*

Gordon Lewis, *Decide for Yourself: A Theological Workbook.*
This book helps you think through Christian doctrines in the context of many alternatives and to work out your own conclusions. *Judge for Yourself* is a similar study.

Paul Steeves, *Getting to Know God.*
———, *Getting to Know Jesus.*
Study guides for personal Bible study.

Frogs,
stop your croaking!
Take cover in the water
and listen to the rain.